Number 156
Winter 2017

New Directions for Evaluation

Leslie A. Fierro
Todd M. Franke
Co Editors-in-Chief

Conducting and Using Evaluative Site Visits

Randi K. Nelson
Denise L. Roseland
Editors

Conducting and Using Evaluative Site Visits
Randi K. Nelson and Denise L. Roseland (eds.)
New Directions for Evaluation, no. 156
Co Editors-in-Chief: *Leslie A. Fierro and Todd M. Franke*

New Directions for Evaluation, (ISSN 1097-6736; Online ISSN: 1534-875X), is published quarterly on behalf of the American Evaluation Association by Wiley Subscription Services, Inc., a Wiley Company, 111 River St., Hoboken, NJ 07030-5774 USA.
Postmaster: Send all address changes to *New Directions for Evaluation*, John Wiley & Sons Inc., C/O The Sheridan Press, PO Box 465, Hanover, PA 17331 USA.

Information for subscribers
New Directions for Evaluation is published in 4 issues per year. Institutional subscription prices for 2017 are:
Print & Online: US$484 (US), US$538 (Canada & Mexico), US$584 (Rest of World), €381 (Europe), £304 (UK). Prices are exclusive of tax. Asia-Pacific GST, Canadian GST/HST and European VAT will be applied at the appropriate rates. For more information on current tax rates, please go to www.wileyonlinelibrary.com/tax-vat. The price includes online access to the current and all online backfiles to January 1st 2013, where available. For other pricing options, including access information and terms and conditions, please visit www.wileyonlinelibrary.com/access.

Delivery Terms and Legal Title
Where the subscription price includes print issues and delivery is to the recipient's address, delivery terms are **Delivered at Place (DAP)**; the recipient is responsible for paying any import duty or taxes. Title to all issues transfers FOB our shipping point, freight prepaid. We will endeavour to fulfil claims for missing or damaged copies within six months of publication, within our reasonable discretion and subject to availability.

Back issues: Single issues from current and recent volumes are available at the current single issue price from cs-journals@wiley.com.

Disclaimer
The Publisher, the American Evaluation Association and Editors cannot be held responsible for errors or any consequences arising from the use of information contained in this journal; the views and opinions expressed do not necessarily reflect those of the Publisher, the American Evaluation Association and Editors, neither does the publication of advertisements constitute any endorsement by the Publisher, the American Evaluation Association and Editors of the products advertised.

Publisher: New Directions for Evaluation is published by Wiley Periodicals, Inc., 350 Main St., Malden, MA 02148-5020.

Journal Customer Services: For ordering information, claims and any enquiry concerning your journal subscription please go to www.wileycustomerhelp.com/ask or contact your nearest office.
Americas: Email: cs-journals@wiley.com; Tel: +1 781 388 8598 or +1 800 835 6770 (toll free in the USA & Canada).
Europe, Middle East and Africa: Email: cs-journals@wiley.com; Tel: +44 (0) 1865 778315.
Asia Pacific: Email: cs-journals@wiley.com; Tel: +65 6511 8000.
Japan: For Japanese speaking support, Email: cs-japan@wiley.com.
Visit our Online Customer Help available in 7 languages at www.wileycustomerhelp.com/ask

Production Editor: Meghanjali Singh (email: mesingh@wiley.com).

Wiley's Corporate Citizenship initiative seeks to address the environmental, social, economic, and ethical challenges faced in our business and which are important to our diverse stakeholder groups. Since launching the initiative, we have focused on sharing our content with those in need, enhancing community philanthropy, reducing our carbon impact, creating global guidelines and best practices for paper use, establishing a vendor code of ethics, and engaging our colleagues and other stakeholders in our efforts. Follow our progress at www.wiley.com/go/citizenship

View this journal online at wileyonlinelibrary.com/journal/ev

Wiley is a founding member of the UN-backed HINARI, AGORA, and OARE initiatives. They are now collectively known as Research4Life, making online scientific content available free or at nominal cost to researchers in developing countries. Please visit Wiley's Content Access - Corporate Citizenship site: http://www.wiley.com/WileyCDA/Section/id-390082.html

Printed in the USA by The Sheridan Group.

Address for Editorial Correspondence: Co Editors-in-chief, Leslie A. Fierro and Todd M. Franke, New Directions for Evaluation, Email: leslie.fierro@cgu.edu, tfranke@g.ucla.edu

Abstracting and Indexing Services
The Journal is indexed by Academic Search Alumni Edition (EBSCO Publishing); Education Research Complete (EBSCO Publishing); Higher Education Abstracts (Claremont Graduate University); SCOPUS (Elsevier); Social Services Abstracts (ProQuest); Sociological Abstracts (ProQuest); Worldwide Political Sciences Abstracts (ProQuest).

Cover design: Wiley
Cover Images: © Lava 4 images | Shutterstock

For submission instructions, subscription and all other information visit:
wileyonlinelibrary.com/journal/ev

Editorial Policy and Procedures

New Directions for Evaluation, a quarterly sourcebook, is an official publication of the American Evaluation Association. The journal publishes works on all aspects of evaluation, with an emphasis on presenting timely and thoughtful reflections on leading-edge issues of evaluation theory, practice, methods, the profession, and the organizational, cultural, and societal context within which evaluation occurs. Each issue of the journal is devoted to a single topic, with contributions solicited, organized, reviewed, and edited by one or more guest editors.

The co editors-in-chief are seeking proposals for journal issues from around the globe about topics new to the journal (although topics discussed in the past can be revisited). A diversity of perspectives and creative bridges between evaluation and other disciplines, as well as chapters reporting original empirical research on evaluation, are encouraged. A wide range of topics and substantive domains are appropriate for publication, including evaluative endeavors other than program evaluation; however, the proposed topic must be of interest to a broad evaluation audience.

Journal issues may take any of several forms. Typically they are presented as a series of related chapters, but they might also be presented as a debate; an account, with critique and commentary, of an exemplary evaluation; a feature-length article followed by brief critical commentaries; or perhaps another form proposed by guest editors.

Submitted proposals must follow the format found via the Association's website at http://www.eval.org/Publications/NDE.asp. Proposals are sent to members of the journal's Editorial Advisory Board and to relevant substantive experts for single-blind peer review. The process may result in acceptance, a recommendation to revise and resubmit, or rejection. The journal does not consider or publish unsolicited single manuscripts.

Before submitting proposals, all parties are asked to contact the co editors-in-chief, who are committed to working constructively with potential guest editors to help them develop acceptable proposals. For additional information about the journal, see the "Statement of the Co Editors-in-Chief" in the Fall 2017, Issue 155.Revis.

Leslie A. Fierro, Co Editors-in-Chief
Assistant Clinical Professor of Evaluation
Claremont Graduate University
Division of Organizational and Behavioral Sciences
Leslie.Fierro@cgu.edu

Todd M. Franke, Co Editors-in-Chief
UCLA
Department of Social Welfare
tfranke@g.ucla.edu

CONTENTS

Michael Quinn Patton
Based on reflection on the chapters in this volume and feedback from others, this chapter presents a revised framework for site-visit standards with the use of a quality-assurance approach.

Editors' Notes

A
s the title suggests, this volume of *New Directions for Evaluation* (NDE) is focused on the use of site visits for evaluation. Although site visits are not a new methodology or method of data collection, the evaluation literature contains very little that provides guidance to professional practice outside the context of accreditation. Evaluation journals and evaluation association conferences frequently include articles and presentations highlighting evaluations that collect data through site visits. However, they do not typically address the wider implications of rigor, ethics, and quality of site visits. Government agencies, philanthropic organizations, and some professional associations have published guidelines for conducting site visits. These typically include site-visit plans, questionnaires, and report templates with a focus on site visits in specific organizational and programmatic contexts. They are usually intended for internal use within the organization and therefore are of limited utility to the broader evaluation community. In contrast, the recommendations and discussions in this volume can serve as a guide to a wider range of evaluation constituents who commission, plan, conduct, and use site visits for purposes including, but not limited to, accreditation. This volume provides an accessible compilation of recommendations based on the experiences of its authors who are evaluation commissioners, practitioners, theorists, and methodologists.

The Guiding Literature on Site Visits in Evaluation

Articles published in peer-reviewed journals on the subject of site visits as a method or methodology in evaluation include two articles by Frances Lawrenz and a book chapter and journal article by Michael Quinn Patton, both of whom are contributors to this NDE volume. Lawrenz's most recent article compared two approaches to conducting site visits for evaluating research centers (Lawrenz, Thao, & Johnson, 2012). An earlier article co-authored by Lawrenz presented evidence for describing evaluative site visits as both a method and a methodology (Lawrenz, Keiser, & Lavoie, 2003). Lawrenz's articles created a strong foundation to support further exploration and consideration of what it means to conduct high-quality site visits. Other peer-reviewed journal articles the authors found in preparing the NDE volume proposal include discussions and research on limitations of site visits due to providing advance notice of the site visit (Palackal & Shrum, 2011); comparison of the quality of data collected using site visits, photographs, and written descriptions of ecological impacts of wilderness campsites (Shelby & Harris, 1985); the acceptability of the

New Directions for Evaluation, no. 156, Winter 2017 © 2017 Wiley Periodicals, Inc., and the American Evaluation Association. Published online in Wiley Online Library (wileyonlinelibrary.com) • DOI: 10.1002/ev.20265 process and results of a site-visit protocol for faculty development and identifying infrastructure needs at community-based health-care teaching sites (Malik, Bordman, Regher, & Freeman; 2007); and a review of tools for direct observation to assess the quality of after-school and youth development programs (Yohalem & Wilson-Ahlstrom, 2009). The proposed volume builds on these initial studies and addresses and elaborates the concerns Patton raised about the quality and appropriate use of site visits (Patton, 2015) and a proposed set of standards for site visits (Patton, 2014).

Advancing the Conversation About Professional Standards for Site Visits

The volume provides an overview of site visits as a methodology and recommends strategies to guide the professional practice of evaluators who conduct site visits and those who commission site visits. The volume is based on research and the experience of the authors who are evaluation theorists and evaluation practitioners. The authors provide wide-ranging perspectives on planning and conducting site visits in diverse substantive areas, geographical contexts, and for different purposes.

In this issue, we use the definition of an evaluative site visit as one that involves people with "specific expertise and preparation" who visit a site for "a limited period of time and gather information about an evaluation object ... to prepare testimony addressing the purpose of the site visit" (Lawrenz, Keiser, & Lavoie, 2003). This definition includes, but is not limited to, site visits conducted for accreditation purposes. In Chapter 1, Melissa Chapman Haynes, Nora Murphy, and Michael Quinn Patton offer a guiding typology for site visits. In Chapter 2, practitioners Corey Newhouse, Denise Roseland, and Professor Frances Lawrenz discuss the nature of trade-offs and planning considerations professional evaluators may face when deciding to use evaluative site visits. Stan Capela, well known for his extensive engagement in accreditation sites visits, and Joe Frisino offer a recipe for conducting accreditation site visits in Chapter 3. In Chapter 4, Donna Podems, who has extensive involvement in site visits internationally, offers a cautionary "tale" about site visits used internationally. Randi Nelson conducted original research for Chapter 5, interviewing key informants to get their perspectives on site visits. In Chapter 6, Melissa Chapman Haynes and Ashley Johnson offer advice for training site visitors. Michael Quinn Patton reflects on the volume and proposes a revision to the standards he offered in 2015, which are paraphrased in Table 1 (Patton, 2015). This volume provides specific and experience-based recommendations for improving the quality and utility of site visits for stakeholders at multiple levels. The authors hope it will spur further conversations and research into improving the theory, practice, and use of evaluative site visits.

NEW DIRECTIONS FOR EVALUATION • DOI: 10.1002/ev

Table 1. A Condensed Version of Patton's 2015 Draft Standards for Site Visits

1. Competence	Ensure that site-visit team members have skills and experience in qualitative observation and interviewing. Availability and subject matter expertise does not suffice.
2. Knowledge	For an evaluative site visit, ensure at least one team member, preferably the team leader, has evaluation knowledge and credentials.
3. Preparation	Site visitors should know something about the site being visited based on background materials, briefings, and/or prior experience.
4. Site participation	People at sites should be engaged in planning and preparation for the site visit to minimize disruption to program activities and services.
5. Do no harm	Site-visit stakes can be high, with risks for people and programs. Good intentions, naiveté, and general cluelessness are not excuses. Be alert to what can go wrong and commit as a team to do no harm.
6. Credible fieldwork	People at the site should be involved and informed, but they should not control the information collection in ways that undermine, significantly limit, or corrupt the inquiry. The evaluators should determine the activities observed and people interviewed, and arrange confidential interviews to enhance data quality.
7. Neutrality	An evaluator conducting fieldwork should not have a preformed position on the intervention or the intervention model.
8. Debriefing and feedback	Before departing from the field, key people at the site should be debriefed on highlights of findings and a timeline of when (or if) they will receive an oral or written report of findings.
9. Site review	Those at the site should have an opportunity to respond in a timely way to site visitors' reports, to correct errors and provide an alternative perspective on findings and judgments. Triangulation and a balance of perspectives should be the rule.
10. Follow-up	The agency commissioning the site visit should do some minimal follow-up to assess the quality of the site visit from the perspective of the locals on site.

References

Lawrenz, F., Keiser, N., & Lavoie, B. (2003). Evaluative site visits: A methodological review. *American Journal of Evaluation, 24*, 341–452.

Lawrenz, F., Thao, M., & Johnson, K. (2012). Expert reviews of research centers: The site visit process. *Evaluation and Program Planning, 35*, 390–397.

Malik, R., Bordman, R., Regher, G., & Freeman, R. (2007). Continuous quality improvement and community-based faculty development through an innovative site visit program at one institution. *Academic Medicine, 82*, 465–468.

Palackal, A., & Shrum, W. (2011). Patterns of visitation: Site visits and evaluation in developing areas. *Sociological Bulletin, 60*, 327–345.

Patton, M. Q. (2014). *Qualitative evaluation and research methods: Integrating theory and practice* (3rd ed.). Thousand Oaks, CA: Sage.

Patton, M. Q. (2015). Evaluation in the field: The need for site visit standards. *American Journal of Evaluation, 36*, 444–460.

Shelby, B., & Harris, R. (1985). Comparing methods for determining visitor evaluations of ecological impacts: Site visits, photographs, and written descriptions. *Journal of Leisure Research, 17*, 57–67.

Yohalem, N., & Wilson-Ahlstrom, A., with Fischer, S. & Shinn, M. (2009). *Measuring youth program quality: A guide to assessment tools* (2nd ed.). Washington, DC: The Forum for Youth Investment.

Randi K. Nelson
Denise L. Roseland

RANDI K. NELSON *is the founder of Partners in Evaluation, LLC, an independent evaluation and training consulting firm and adjunct faculty at the University of Minnesota.*

DENISE L. ROSELAND *earned her Ph.D. in Evaluation Studies from the University of Minnesota and is the founder/CEO of ChangeMaker Consulting, an independent consulting firm that works with nonprofits, government agencies, schools, and foundations to be more strategic and achieve greater impact.*

Chapman Haynes, M., Murphy, N. F., & Patton, M. Q. (2017). A guiding typology for site visits. In R. K. Nelson & D. L. Roseland (Eds.), *Conducting and Using Evaluative Site Visits. New Directions for Evaluation*, 156, 11–19.

1

A Guiding Typology for Site Visits

Melissa Chapman Haynes ⒾⒹ, *Nora F. Murphy,*
Michael Quinn Patton ⒾⒹ

Abstract

Site visits are an often-implemented, understudied activity that occurs in the diverse contexts where program evaluation is conducted. Further, the purposes of evaluative site visits are varied, ranging from provision of technical assistance and formative learning to high-stakes accreditation site visits. The purpose of this chapter is to set the stage for the rest of this New Directions for Evaluation volume by presenting a typology of site visits with examples that illustrate variations in the eight categories or characteristics of the proposed typology. The typology will help practitioners clarify their thinking around their own site visits and aid in the evaluation planning and design phase of their practice. Additional chapters in this volume will add to the typology by discussing various aspects of quality, procedures, and use of site visits. © 2017 Wiley Periodicals, Inc., and the American Evaluation Association.

In the early 2000s, a large, federally funded, politically charged early literacy program called Early Reading First was being launched as part of the larger No Child Left Behind legislation. Awardees of this program were required to secure an external evaluation, as well as participate in the national evaluation of the program, which included an annual site visit. Melissa Chapman Haynes was part of the external evaluation team for a grantee in a rural Midwestern state. This was fortunate because this would be a first foray into on-the-ground training in site visits, which is the norm for evaluators, as there is little mention of site visits in evaluation texts or chapters for students or practitioners. The site visit from the national evaluation team included the perspectives of the program staff, which were the primary focus of the site visit, and that of the external evaluation team.

At the same time, in a different part of the country, Nora Murphy, new to the evaluation field, was part of the Youth Standards Project. This initiative sought to develop a set of youth standards designed by and for youth-serving organizations with the intention of raising the quality of services available to youth and creating a common set of expectations for funders. Murphy worked with a team of evaluators and organizational staff to develop a site-visit protocol that would allow organizations and funders to use the standards to guide evaluations.

The details of these particular site visits are less important than the overall takeaway lessons learned from what were very stressful experiences, particularly for our clients running the program. They learned that site visits are often time-consuming, to some degree anxiety-provoking, and politically charged. In Chapman Haynes' experience, the particular site visit did not add value to the evaluation and did not seem to have any effect on the program beyond the preparation beforehand to showcase the best aspects of the program. In Murphy's experience, the tension between uniform expectations for conducting site visits and the need for contextual adaptations became clear.

Defining evaluative site visits is a formidable challenge, not only because they occur in diverse contexts for an array of purposes, but also because there is very little in the evaluation literature to serve as guidance (Lawrenz, Keiser, & Lavoie, 2003; Patton, 2015). The purpose of this chapter is to provide a framework for the types of evaluative site visits that occur, based on a literature review as well as our collective experiences as evaluators. It is our hope that this chapter and volume will spur conversations and further investigations into evaluative site visits and provide guidance for evaluators participating in, planning, or implementing site visits.

Construction and Boundaries of the Typology

Perhaps Alfred Nobel can provide some guidance to our development of a site-visit typology, as he said "One can state, without exaggeration, that the observation of and search for similarities and differences are the basis of all human knowledge" (Frängsmyr, 1996). The process of identifying typologies in qualitative sociological research is focused on identifying unique dimensions that are similar within group and distinct between groups (Kluge, 2000). This typology was constructed based on our personal and collective experiences as professional evaluators and a literature review from the fields of program evaluation, anthropology, sociology, education, health care, and international development.

Given that there is very little general guidance about the methods for conducting site visits in the literature, the review focused on providing examples, context, and exemplars to support the typology presented in this chapter. Further, during the literature review it became apparent that evaluative site visits are also referred to as field studies (Nightingale & Rosman, 2015), implementation studies (U.S. Department of Labor, 2012), or as field work. Our literature search included these terms. We will use the term *site visits* throughout this chapter to refer to all these types of studies.

What cannot be captured in a typology are the important roles that context, culture, and credibility play in site visits. Any type of site visit can happen in a school, clinic, or health care setting. But how should evaluators think about and attend to variations of context? The cultures of a clinic for military veterans, elderly nursing home residents, or youth experiencing homelessness will vary greatly. How does the site visit attend to these variations? What makes the site visit credible—from evaluator, to methods, to findings?

Typology

Site visits are conducted for a wide range of purposes that vary in the questions they seek to answer, when they happen in the life course of the program or initiative, what is at stake, and the degree to which the protocol is standardized or contextually specific. Based on a review of the literature and our personal experiences with site visits, we present a proposed typology with eight dimensions on which site visits may vary in a meaningful manner (Figure 1.1). We also present and discuss a continuum for each dimension. For example, "Nature of site engagement" can range from entirely externally directed to collaborative or participatory.

Each dimension is further detailed in the following sections with examples of site visits that fit within the continuum.

Degree of Standardization

The first dimension in the typology ranges from exploratory site visits, which have no standardized protocol, to accreditation visits in which the site visitors follow a highly standardized and detailed protocol. Between the extremes are visits that may be customized to a specific context and those that are semistructured. An example of a semistructured visit would be when the evaluator and program leaders identify individuals the site-visit team will interview and meet and the nature of those meetings is generally agreed upon but the processes and line of questioning are left somewhat open. A customized site-visit example is one in which an external evaluator is asked to conduct annual site visits to plan and facilitate logic modeling exercises with key program stakeholders as part of the broader evaluation planning and data collection.

NEW DIRECTIONS FOR EVALUATION • DOI: 10.1002/ev

Figure 1.1. Site-visit typology dimensions, definitions, and proposed categories.

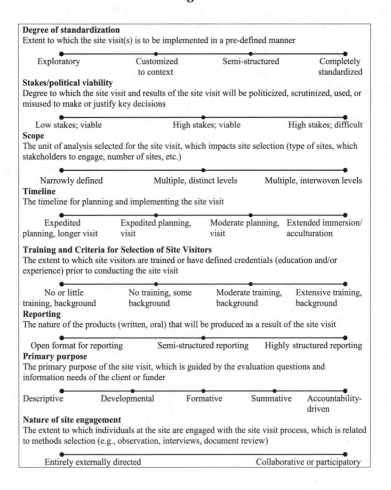

Degree of standardization
Extent to which the site visit(s) is to be implemented in a pre-defined manner

Exploratory — Customized to context — Semi-structured — Completely standardized

Stakes/political viability
Degree to which the site visit and results of the site visit will be politicized, scrutinized, used, or misused to make or justify key decisions

Low stakes; viable — High stakes; viable — High stakes; difficult

Scope
The unit of analysis selected for the site visit, which impacts site selection (type of sites, which stakeholders to engage, number of sites, etc.)

Narrowly defined — Multiple, distinct levels — Multiple, interwoven levels

Timeline
The timeline for planning and implementing the site visit

Expedited planning, longer visit — Expedited planning, visit — Moderate planning, visit — Extended immersion/acculturation

Training and Criteria for Selection of Site Visitors
The extent to which site visitors are trained or have defined credentials (education and/or experience) prior to conducting the site visit

No or little training, background — No training, some background — Moderate training, background — Extensive training, background

Reporting
The nature of the products (written, oral) that will be produced as a result of the site visit

Open format for reporting — Semi-structured reporting — Highly structured reporting

Primary purpose
The primary purpose of the site visit, which is guided by the evaluation questions and information needs of the client or funder

Descriptive — Developmental — Formative — Summative — Accountability-driven

Nature of site engagement
The extent to which individuals at the site are engaged with the site visit process, which is related to methods selection (e.g., observation, interviews, document review)

Entirely externally directed — Collaborative or participatory

Exploratory site visits are likely to be conducted when little is known about how program activities or an organization is operating. In this context it would not be appropriate or feasible to develop a highly standardized protocol. As an example, a series of exploratory site visits may be conducted for grantees that are given a small amount of funding to improve nutrition policies and practices in schools. The site-visit team may develop overall goals and guiding questions for the visit, but unless specific guidance or standards were provided to each grantee it would not be possible (or even appropriate) to develop highly standardized protocols.

The most highly standardized site visits may be accreditation visits, which are typically highly structured. For example, the Accreditation Council for Graduate Medical Education (ACGME) details specific steps the site visitor must take as part of a site visit, including a review of program requirements and data that are submitted to the site-visit team prior to the in-person visit; interviews with the program director, faculty members, and residents; and review of the available data that were submitted prior to the site visit to verify and expand on that information.

The Council on Accreditation, an international nonprofit with a mission to develop and support accreditation of human services organizations, defines accreditation as "the formal evaluation of an organization or program against best practice standards" (Council on Accreditation website, June 1, 2016). Accreditation is defined as both a status and a process and typically involves a rigorous and standardized site-visit protocol.

Stakes and Political Viability

The second dimension focuses on the stakes of the site visit and includes the political viability of conducting the site visit itself as well as the impact of political pressures to misuse results. This dimension deals with the context and politics of the site visit, including the purpose of the site visit, who has requested or commissioned it, who will use the results, and how results might be used. Other factors that influence stakes and political viability include the potential for misuse of results and the competing interests of stakeholders, including funders and key decision makers.

At one end of the continuum are site visits with low stakes that are politically viable, meaning there is little evidence that the results will be used to make high-stakes decisions by the entity commissioning the visit, that there is a lower likelihood that results will be misused, and there is general support for the site visit among various stakeholders and key leaders. One example of such a visit would be a site visit for a broadly supported, adequately funded community health initiative, where the purpose of the site visit is to gather information through a variety of methods for program improvement. Although we can never entirely control or predict how results will be used, the focus at this end of the continuum is on improvement.

At the other end of the continuum there are site visits that have higher stakes, which may be either politically viable or challenging. Yarbrough, Shulha, Hopson, and Caruthers (2011) identified two sets of factors that should be considered when defining the context and ultimately the feasibility of conducting an evaluation or an evaluative site visit. The first set of factors is broader political influences at play, including economics, religious, and cultural values. The second set of factors is the background values individuals involved in the site visit bring to the site visit. It is the responsibility of the evaluator to engage in activities that will shed light on the stakes of the evaluation and the feasibility of conducting the site visit within the identified political context.

NEW DIRECTIONS FOR EVALUATION • DOI: 10.1002/ev

Scope

The third dimension, scope, involves the unit of analysis for the site visit. Site visits may be narrowly defined, attending to a preidentified component of the program or stakeholder group, or may be focused on multiple levels of an organization or multiple partners or stakeholder groups. Defining the scope necessarily defines some of the practical aspects of the site visits, including the number and type of individuals who will be involved, the depth of data collection and analysis, and the selection of methods. It may be the case that resources constrain the scope of a site visit to the extent that it is only possible to have a narrow focus, including only one level of an organization or a couple of stakeholder groups in an interview. However, a narrow focus may jeopardize the feasibility of the site visit, particularly if an interested group is excluded from providing input into the evaluation, and hence may ultimately resist the site visit and the evaluation, making it less feasible to implement.

Timeline

The fourth dimension concerns the time available for planning and implementing the site visit, ranging from expedited timelines to those that span an extended period of time. As noted by Patton (2014, 2015) it is too often the case that the timeline for site visits is brief. In some cases there are only weeks between the deadline for the request for proposal or other call for site visitors and the start of the contract. This compact timeline may increase the likelihood that unqualified site visitors will be hired, as many more qualified or experienced site visitors are not able to respond to the timeline or travel on such short notice.

Patton (2015) also noted that it is most commonly the case that the length of the site visit itself is brief, typically lasting a few days at most. In some contexts, a longer site visit may increase the accuracy and utility of information gained, especially in contexts that involve wicked problems or highly complex systems. This approach would be more akin to anthropological approaches such as ethnography. Although there are benefits to longer site visits, there is also tension between utility and accuracy of the visit and the feasibility of doing more extended site visits, given the available resources and the information needs of the stakeholders.

Because of the high cost of site visits, especially if considering extending the length of a site visit, it may be worthwhile to consider what we might learn from studying participant observation, an anthropological method that typically involves extended observation and data collection. It involves "going out and staying out ... and experiencing the lives of the people you are studying as much as you can" (Bernard, 2006, p. 344). It usually involves collection of qualitative information, such as observations, and may also include collection of quantitative data. And although this method originated in cultural anthropological studies of remote tribes, it is also used today to study areas with direct application, such as a study in the early 1990s about why consumers were not using credit card readers at gas stations (Solomon, 1993).

Training and Criteria for Selection of Site Visitors

The fifth dimension, training, consists of two components. First is the specific training that the site visitor might receive prior to conducting the site visit. Second are the credentials that the site visitor or the site-visit team may need to have, which may consider level of education and experience. At one end of the continuum there may be no stated requirements for training or background of the site visitor.

As a next step on the continuum, a site visit may require no specific training but there may be requirements for the site visitor's education or experience related to the context of the site visit. For example, requirements for an advanced degree in a particular field of study, practical experience within a certain context (e.g., as a teacher, in international contexts, working with specific populations), or years of experience conducting evaluations or evaluative site visits.

Sometimes there are requirements that the site visitor or team have extensive training as well as specific background or experience in a particular context or field. For example, the ACGME staff members who serve as site visitors must have ACGME-provided site-visit training. They are required to have extensive experience in the field of medical education, typically part of MD or PhD degree-granting programs; they must participate in two formal meetings each year; and attend specific meetings each year to maintain their credentials to conduct these site visits.

Reporting

The sixth dimension focuses on the nature of the tasks or products that will be delivered as a result of the site visit, including oral reports, written reports, or any summary of the process or findings of the visit. The extent to which reports and other deliverables are publicly available (or not) is also a consideration for this dimension. On one end of the continuum the nature of the reporting may be open with no required format for the reporting. A semistructured format seems to be most common for reporting the process and findings of the site visit. Site visits that evaluators conduct as a requirement of the funder or a request of the client are often structured. The evaluator typically writes a summary that includes the activities conducted during the site visit and the findings. There is often little additional required format beyond a deliverable deadline. On the other end of the spectrum, accreditation reporting is often highly structured, including checklists of activities that must be completed, standardized report formats that may include structured rubrics, and required details about the findings. Whether the format is open to customization or highly structured, it is

NEW DIRECTIONS FOR EVALUATION • DOI: 10.1002/ev

essential that site visit reports take into consideration the audience receiving reports and the intended use of the information, particularly the extent to which reports will be made public and the extent to which publicly available reports will be easy or difficult to access.

Primary Purpose

The seventh dimension should be driven by the information needs of the client and stakeholders, whether it is formally detailed in a structured manner prior to the site visit or something that the site-visit team needs to establish prior to the visit. Purposes may be descriptive, developmental, formative, summative, or focused on accountability—or some combination of these purposes. A descriptive site visit describes what is, what isn't, where it's happening, and where it isn't. The primary purpose is to describe and document, either for the site itself, the external agency requiring the site visit, or both. A developmental site has the purpose of documenting what is useful to support the development of an innovation or something being adapted to a new and novel context. A formative site visit is conducted during program development to identify when it is not being delivered as planned or not having the intended effects to modify the intervention accordingly. A summative site visit generally provides feedback to stakeholders at the end of the program or renders a judgment such as whether a site should be accredited.

Nature of Site Engagement

Finally, the nature of site engagement may range from those that are entirely directed externally with little engagement of the individuals on site beyond meetings or interviews to those that are highly collaborative and participatory. Accreditation visits tend to have less engagement with individuals at the site beyond observation of certain activities or programs in action or interviews with specified individuals. On the other hand, site visits that are conducted for the purposes of facilitating an activity toward the development of logic models will be much more collaborative in nature. Those at the site may be involved with providing input on the individuals or groups that should be involved and the design and implementation of activities on-site. The nature of engagement is highly related to the purpose and to whether the actual process of asking people to engage in the site visit is intended to stimulate change in the program, intervention, or initiative. As we move forward with applying this typology, it may be useful to learn from prior studies of process use (Shaw & Campbell, 2013) and how this may translate into our understanding of how individuals at the site being visited are affected by participating in an evaluative site visit.

Next Steps

The typology proposed in this chapter will be referenced and put into action throughout this volume. Future work that collects data toward refining or revising this typology will be an essential step in moving this work forward. It is our hope that the proposed typology serves as an initial framework in a broader conversation about site visits and that it will be refined and reworked as it is systematically held up against the practice of conducting site visits.

References

Bernard, H. R. (2006). *Research methods in anthropology: Qualitative and quantitative approaches*. Oxford, United Kingdom: AltaMira.

Council on Accreditation. *The cornerstone of COA accreditation*. Retrieved from http://coanet.org/standards/standards-overview. Accessed June 1, 2016

Frängsmyr, T. (1996). *Alfred Nobel—Life and philosophy*. Retrieved from https://www.nobelprize.org/alfred_nobel/biographical/articles/frangsmyr/

Kluge, S. (2000). Empirically grounded construction of types and typologies in qualitative social research. *Forum Qualitative Sozialforschung/Forum: Qualitative Social Research*, 1(1). Retrieved from http://nbn-resolving.de/urn:nbn:de:0114-fqs0001145

Lawrenz, F., Keiser, N., & Lavoie, B. (2003). Evaluative site visits: A methodological review. *American Journal of Evaluation*, 24, 341–352.

Nightingale, D. S., & Rosman, S. B. (2015). Collecting data in the field. In K. E. Newcomer, H. P. Hatry, & J. S. Wholey (Eds.), *Handbook of practical program evaluation* (4th ed.). Hoboken, NJ: John Wiley & Sons.

Patton, M. Q. (2014). *Qualitative evaluation and research methods: Integrating theory and practice* (4th ed.). Thousand Oaks, CA: Sage.

Patton, M. Q. (2015). Evaluation in the field: The need for site visit standards. *American Journal of Evaluation*, 36, 444–460.

Shaw, J., & Campbell, R. (2013). The "process" of process use methods for longitudinal assessment in a multisite evaluation. *American Journal of Evaluation*, 35, 250–260.

Solomon, C. (1993, August 4). Transportation: Self-service at gas stations includes paying. *The Wall Street Journal*, p. B1.

U.S. Department of Labor, Clearinghouse for Labor Evaluation and Research (CLEAR). (2012). *Operational guidelines for reviewing implementation studies*. Retrieved from https://www.dol.gov/asp/evaluation/resources/operational_implementation_study_guidelines.pdf

Yarbrough, D. B., Shulha, L. M., Hopson, R. K., & Caruthers, F. A. (2011). *The program evaluation standards: A guide for evaluators and evaluation users*. Thousand Oaks, CA: Sage.

MELISSA CHAPMAN HAYNES *is a senior evaluator at Professional Data Analysts in Minneapolis, MN.*

NORA MURPHY *is a founding member and president of TerraLuna Collaborative in Minneapolis, MN.*

MICHAEL QUINN PATTON *is the founder and director of Utilization Focused Evaluation in St. Paul, MN.*

Newhouse, C., Roseland, D., Lawrenz, F. (2017). Site visits: Conversations for practice. In R. K. Nelson & D. L. Roseland (Eds.), *Conducting and Using Evaluative Site Visits. New Directions for Evaluation, 156*, 21–32.

2

Site Visits: Conversations for Practice

Corey Newhouse, Denise Roseland ⓘⒹ *, Frances Lawrenz* ⓘⒹ

Abstract

The existence of multiple purposes for site visits can explain some of the variation seen in the design and use of site visits in practice. In some instances, site visits are one element of a larger evaluation design where results are blended with data from a variety of sources. In other instances, site visits stand alone as the entire evaluation. This chapter discusses three case studies from the perspective of evaluation practitioners that are aligned with the typology presented in the previous chapter by Chapman Haynes, Murphy, and Patton. They illustrate three distinct conditions where site visits have been used in evaluation. The cases selected include two site visits that are part of a suite of numerous evaluation activities that comprise the evaluation design and one case where the site visit comprises the entire evaluation. The chapter concludes with five crosscutting themes that form practical considerations for incorporating site visits into evaluation practice. © 2017 Wiley Periodicals, Inc., and the American Evaluation Association.

The Varying Roles Site Visits May Play in Evaluation

To lay the groundwork for the discussion that follows in this chapter, it is important to acknowledge the varying purposes site visits may play in overall evaluation design. The purpose for site visits illustrated by the cases described in this chapter includes use of site visits for (a) compliance monitoring of multisite programs, (b) assessing quality of program implementation and program outcomes, and (c) evaluating the quality of a university research center. We offer these cases to challenge evaluation practitioners to leverage the power of site visits to add value and to deliver lessons learned, actionable findings, and value. We have italicized the dimensions of the typology referenced in the previous chapter by Chapman Haynes, Murphy, and Patton as we discuss those dimensions in the case study.

Case One: Compliance Monitoring of Multisite Programs

Multisite programs are programs conducted or replicated simultaneously at a number of sites. Multisite programs are often required to participate in routine site visits intended to monitor program implementation for compliance with programmatic, legislative, or funding requirements. These externally defined requirements generally determine the *degree of standardization* of a compliance-monitoring site visit, which are often semistructured or customized to the program's context. When site visits are used for compliance-monitoring purposes, efforts often focus on the assembly and collection of data to examine specific elements of a program such as its fiscal, staffing, or operational procedures. However, site visits for compliance monitoring may not have the breadth, depth, or methodological rigor of a full program evaluation. Compliance-oriented site visits may or may not be a part of a larger evaluation and in some instances the site visit combined with other programmatic records constitutes the entire evaluation.

Site visits for compliance monitoring can be used for a number of *purposes,* which include

- allowing analysis of data across and within sites during program implementation for formative purposes;
- assuring accountability to a funder, governing body, and the public;
- engaging in program advocacy by protecting or advancing the interests of stakeholders among funders, governing agencies, the public; and
- supporting decision-making for future resource allocations or awarding of future funds.

The *nature of site engagement* for a site visit for compliance monitoring varies considerably when measured by the site visit's duration, structure, activities conducted, and parties involved. Although evaluators may choose to develop their own rubric or checklist for data collection, the organization requiring the compliance monitoring often sets the *scope* by providing rules, regulations, and standards to be measured during the site visit. In addition, the organization requiring the visit will often provide *training* and guidance regarding the methodology and process to be used. Most often, the *site visitors* conducting the site visit are subject-matter experts or organizational leaders associated with the agency requiring the compliance monitoring. They are not usually neutral third parties. *Timelines* to conduct

New Directions for Evaluation • DOI: 10.1002/ev

site visits for compliance monitoring vary considerably but rarely involve extended immersion or longer visits. *Reporting* the results from compliance-monitoring site visits is often highly structured—usually in the form of a written report that features findings related to the criteria, standards, and expectations of the organization that commissions the site visits. *Stakes* for compliance-monitoring visits are often high, potentially resulting in sanctions for noncompliance or findings that would threaten eligibility for current or future funding.

Compliance-Monitoring Site-Visit Example

The U.S. Department of Education (USDoE): Carl D. Perkins Career and Technical Education Improvement Act of 2006 requires state agencies that administer funds associated with this legislation to monitor local recipients to assure compliance with fiscal and management requirements of the legislation. Local recipients of funds include school districts and career and technical post-secondary education programs. Funds are awarded based on a detailed proposal and guided by formulas that assure equitable use of funds for targeted subpopulations of students, which may be defined by gender, race/ethnicity, or being economically disadvantaged. Local recipients are responsible for achieving negotiated performance standards on federally determined indicators through measurement approaches among programs and states.

The USDoE offers guidance to state agencies on how to monitor compliance, but each state determines its own process and data collection tools. Most states use site visits as a part of monitoring for compliance. Some states conduct routine site visits to all recipients on a rotating basis, and other states conduct targeted site visits based on below-standard performance as determined by a desk audit. A few states conduct no in-person site visits but instead monitor compliance using other data collection methods such as surveys, online reporting tools, and fiscal record reviews. In all cases, other sources of data and information are used to supplement data collected during site visits. These typically include financial and staffing data, programmatic data (i.e., participant data, institutional data, area workforce data), interviews, and surveys.

Program staff members at the state agencies that administer the federal funds conduct the site visits. Results are reported annually to the USDoE by the state agencies. The USDoE makes reported findings available to Congress and the public—via its website and in response to requests—to document appropriate use of public resources. The state agency staff uses the compliance-monitoring site-visit findings to guide and inform technical assistance provided to local recipients and to make future allocation decisions. In some instances, fiscal or management sanctions can result from negative findings. Local recipients use findings from site visits to remedy compliance issues before the program reapplies for funding during the next award cycle.

This example demonstrates how the design and use of a site visit plays out in compliance-monitoring practice and highlights that even with a compliance-monitoring purpose, evaluators still make important decisions regarding the design and implementation of site visits as a part of an evaluation.

Case Two: Observations of Point-of-Service Quality

This case discusses another role for site visits in evaluation: observing program quality. Site visits are an effective approach for collecting robust information about point-of-service quality. Point-of-service quality is distinct from other forms of program quality, such as an organization's financial health, staff hiring and support practices, or curriculum because it focuses on the observable features of the program environment. These features may include the interactions among staff and clients or opportunities for extended engagement with subject-specific content (Smith, Devaney, Akiva, & Sugar, 2009). In most cases, the observational data collected through the site visits are then filtered through a rubric or checklist to determine the extent to which the observed program aligns with research-based best practices.

Although evaluators may choose to develop their own observation rubric or checklist, many pre-existing tools are well suited to this purpose. Adopting or adapting an existing validated observation tool adds rigor to the evaluation design and is more efficient than developing a new or original tool. In the youth development field, compendia such as Measuring Youth Program Quality (Yohalem, Wilson-Ahlstrom, Fischer, & Shinn, 2009) provide in-depth reviews of available observational tools.

There are three primary benefits to using point-of-service quality–focused site visits. First, focusing on point-of-service quality is a client-centered approach to evaluation, focusing on the lived experience of the program participants. This brings the importance of clients' experiences to the forefront of evaluation practice. Second, point-of-service observations can identify existing gaps between what the program is intended to do and how it actually operates in practice. This information can highlight both critical gaps in programmatic implementation, as well as to identify unplanned innovations. Third, point-of-service quality–focused site visits allow evaluators to compare and contrast somewhat dissimilar programs. The use of a common metric of point-of-service quality allows evaluators to document the extent to which foundational elements are present across a variety of settings. This approach can help guide investments in cross-site staff training, for example, or help funders compare the performance of a group of programs.

New Directions for Evaluation • DOI: 10.1002/ev

Depending on the intended *purpose* of the evaluation, point-of-service quality–focused site visits can be used *formatively*, to provide input to practitioners about the strength of their practice or for *accountability* purposes, such as ensuring that a group of program sites are consistently implementing mandated practices. Generally speaking, the *stakes* for point-of-service–focused site visits are low, especially if the visit is conducted for formative purposes, because the purpose of formative visits is to provide performance feedback to the staff running the program. Sometimes the *stakes* for point-of-service site visits are higher, such as when they are part of a funder-commissioned evaluation. When the *stakes* for visits are high, evaluators should adopt a high level of *standardization* in the visits and consistent *reporting* protocols. To assure consistent process, evaluators should conduct rigorous training for visitors conducting high-stakes site visits, especially if the results will be compared across program sites or organizations. The *timeline* for point-of-service quality site visits depends on their intended use. In a formative setting, the evaluator may want to conduct visits fairly early in the program development cycle. In a summative context, the evaluator should consider visiting when the program is more established. It is ideal to conduct two to three point-of-service–focused visits per program cycle, subject to budget constraints.

Point-of-Service Quality Site-Visit Example

The Oakland Fund for Children and Youth (OFCY) was created in 1996 through a voter initiative that sought to use city funds to support direct services for children from birth through 21 years. OFCY makes between 100 and 150 grants per 3-year funding cycle to programs serving children and youth in a wide variety of settings, including schools, recreation centers, parks, and housing communities. Although grantees share broad goals, such as providing safe and engaging after-school programming or helping youth build workforce skills, each funded program has its own staffing, curriculum, and client base. The OFCY sought an evaluation approach that would allow its staff and board to compare grantees particularly regarding the quality of programming supported by public funds. Public Profit, an evaluation consultancy specializing in youth and family programs, served as OFCY's evaluator.

OFCY's grant guidelines for programs serving school-aged (6–18 years) and transition-aged youth (16–21 years) include a focus on positive youth development practices (Oakland Fund for Children and Youth, 2014). Positive youth development practices formed the common thread the evaluation team used for point-of-service quality observations. Public Profit used the Program Quality Assessment (PQA) from the David P. Weikart Center for Youth Program Quality to structure the point-of-service–focused visits. The Program Quality Assessment is a validated observational instrument aligned with core principles of positive youth development. The PQA is used by

NEW DIRECTIONS FOR EVALUATION • DOI: 10.1002/ev

after-school and youth service organizations across the United States. For the OFCY evaluation, Public Profit used the PQA to conduct point-of-service quality observations during a 4-month period in the fall and early winter during each year of implementation. Programs were grouped into three categories based on their PQA score: Emerging, Performing, or Thriving. Programs scoring in the Emerging category (i.e., those with low point-of-service visit scores) were required to develop a plan to address the issues identified in the site visit and to share it with site-level stakeholders and OFCY.

Site-visit reports are typically shared with program staff and OFCY within a few weeks of the visit. Score summaries for each observed program are included in publicly available reports about the OFCY's grant strategy, which are issued twice per year. Site-visit results are used at the program level to inform shifts in program design, staffing, and training. OFCY uses the results to identify and publicize high-performing grantees and to identify programs in need of additional support.

This example demonstrates how point-of-service–focused site visits can support two distinct purposes—continuous quality improvement and grant monitoring. Key components of these visits, including the use of a common site-visit tool, consistent reporting criteria, well-trained visitors, and quick return of site-visit reports to programs, all reflect a desire to balance these two purposes.

Case Three: Assessing Research Center Quality

One important use of site visits is to assess the quality of interdisciplinary research centers. These centers provide space for researchers from different disciplines to come together to solve grand societal challenges. These types of research centers have been enjoying increased federal funding, such as the National Science Foundation's Science of Learning Centers grants and the National Institutes for Health's Clinical Translational Science awards. The Government Accountability Office (GAO) found that expert panel review and site visits were frequently used in evaluating federal program performance for all federal programs (GAO, 2003). In terms of validity, expert panel review is viewed as the gold standard for ascertaining research quality and other assessment methods are often compared to it (Butler & McAllister, 2011; Rons, DeBruyn & Cornelis, 2011). Generally, this type of site visit is conducted by a team of experts who provide a connoisseurship approach to evaluation (Eisner, 1998) and follow procedures outlined in Lawrenz, Thao, and Johnson (2012). The rest of this section describes a recent site visit to a research center at a major research university following the dimensions presented in the typology in the previous chapter of this volume.

New Directions for Evaluation • DOI: 10.1002/ev

Research Center Quality Site-Visit Example

This case is an evaluative site visit of a large interdisciplinary social science research center at a major university. The center is well funded with external grants and reports directly to the Office of the Vice President for Research for the university overall. It has been in operation for 15 years. There is a large staff of research scientists as well as affiliated faculty. Excluding faculty members with part-time appointments, the center employs 185 staff members including 32 researchers, 24 software developers and other IT professionals, 19 technical specialist and data processors, 7 administrative staff, and 96 research assistants. Because of its rapid growth, the center is in the process of reorganization into different divisions under a more hierarchical framework. The center is guided in all of its actions by an active Advisory Board, which meets monthly. The Advisory Board members are elected by the members of the center and include three categories of representatives: faculty, center research scientists, and graduate and postdoctoral scholars. Each is elected by a different constituency of center members. The founder of the center and its original director remains the director today. Its four core areas are administrative, development, scientific/technical, and public.

The *timeline* for the site visit was approximately 6 months, starting from the determination of the need for the site visit to the completion of the visit and the submission of the final report. The center used the 6 months to prepare a comprehensive self-study for use by the site visitors. The self-study included descriptions of all center processes, personnel, and outcomes, such as grants and publications. The scheduling of the visit took place early in the process to accommodate work schedules of the site visitors. The results of the self-study were sent to the site-visit team 2 weeks before the scheduled visit. The visit itself took 2 1/2 days. The site visitors met with the Vice President for Research the evening before the site visit formally began to discuss the goals of the site visit. In this case the main goal was to describe strengths and weaknesses of the center and to make suggestions for strengthening it. The next day the visitors engaged in a series of meetings with the different types of people associated with the center. They conducted interviews with the Center Director, directors of other affiliated centers at the University, graduate students, faculty members, research scientist staff at the center, the faculty member in charge of training for the center, the directors of the various divisions of the center and the deans and department heads of entities associated with the center. Site visitors also observed the center's facilities. The site visitors discussed center operation with the center Advisory Board members over lunch. The visitors had the evening and the next morning to prepare their report, which they delivered orally to the Center Director and the Vice President for Research at lunchtime. They finished their written report before departing. The center shared the results with the center's Advisory Board, which approves center operations.

New Directions for Evaluation • DOI: 10.1002/ev

The site visit was *customized to the context* of the center in terms of the types of people they interviewed and the type of data they examined. The site visitors were asked if there were anything specific they wished to see or do and those requests were incorporated into the visit schedule along with items the site and the sponsor felt were important. There was no specific *report* framework. The site visitors were allowed to use whatever format fit their ideas except that there had to be an oral and a written report. They organized the report around several themes that they saw in the self-study data and from their interviews and observations. They discussed these orally and answered questions from the Center Director and the Vice President for Research. This allowed clarification of any misunderstandings about their findings. After this presentation they finalized their ideas into an 11-page report with five themes and specific recommendations for leadership, training, sustainability, visibility, and faculty development.

The site visitors provided their opinions based on their existing background knowledge combined with what they learned from the self-study and the day of meetings on site. They had to be very carefully selected, because the validity of the site visit was dependent on their expertise. To accomplish this, lists were developed of potential visitors who had a broad range of expertise covering the research conducted in the center. Three visitors were selected by the Vice President for Research from this list and invited to conduct the site visit. They were *selected* to be from diverse locations and types of centers as well as to have diverse expertise. No specific *training* or preparation other than reading the self-study was required.

The site visit had somewhat *high stakes* and was intended to be both summative and formative. If the site-visit results had been negative, the center could possibly be closed. However, in this case the center was clearly doing very well, so it was highly unlikely the results would be negative. The site visit was more an administrative requirement to follow an-every-5-years review process that all research centers had to follow. The *purpose* of the visit was mostly formative, helping to point out how the center could become even better.

Evaluative site visits to research centers are a distinctive type of site visits. Research by its very nature is unique, so it would be impossible to have detailed standardized questions that would cover all instances of visits to a variety of research centers. The actual conduct of research at the center needs to be explored in depth and compared to best practices in the various disciplines involved. Understanding the research and its impact usually requires deep disciplinary knowledge. Some generic questions are possible, such as efficiency of operation, number of publications and grants, or general topical areas such as those emerging from this visit (leadership, training, sustainability, visibility, and faculty development). However, it is the degree to which the center is performing on these criteria within its specific research arena that is the variable of interest, and that is not generic. That question can only be answered by experts in the field. Also, it is relatively uncommon for comparative evaluations of groups of the same type of research center to occur, so consistency in data gathered across visits is less of an issue.

Practical Considerations When Incorporating Site Visits Into an Evaluation Design

As the cases in this chapter illustrate, site visits can play a variety of purposes in an evaluation. We identified five cross-cutting themes based on our experience using site visits. They are presented here as five interconnected considerations for evaluation teams to take into account when planning an evaluation. The use of site visits as a part of evaluation is neither easy nor foolproof. In spite of its limitations, an evaluator who pays careful attention to the trade-offs inherent in the design of a site visit can still gather and harness powerful information for the evaluation. These considerations are by no means exhaustive. We have, however, found them to be most useful in successfully incorporating site visits into a variety of evaluation designs.

Consideration 1: What Is the Unique Role a Site Visit Plays in an Evaluation?

Site visits represent a substantial investment of time and money, both on the part of the evaluator and on the evaluee. It is therefore essential to consider the role a site visit plays in the overall evaluation design—whether part of a larger evaluation design or as the evaluation in its entirety. As such, the data collected through a site visit must be intimately tied to the intended use of the findings. The planning consideration that matters most is this question: "Does the use of site visits deliver unique value to whoever commissions the evaluation and to the site being visited?". If the answer is yes, then evaluators should proceed with additional planning considerations related to budgeting for the cost of site visits, the time to prepare for and conduct site visits, and other process-related considerations. However, if it is unclear whether a site visit can truly add value, then evaluators must more thoroughly explore the merits of site visits relative to other methodologies.

The cases highlight how differing definitions of quality and forms of proof influence the design of a site visit. In some instances, the goal is for site visitors to reach consensus or demonstrate reliability in ratings (normalized views) as they arrive at a single determination of quality. In others, the diversity of viewpoints of experts is not only acceptable but also desirable. Evaluation planners must clearly understand the conditions in which these different approaches make sense and add value. Planning for site visits where normalized views are valuable (i.e., consensus among raters or interrater reliability) means planning adequate time, training, and budget to deliver these kinds of results. In contrast, planning for site visits that require and value differing views among experts requires investing resources in assembling a diverse and highly qualified team capable of delivering those findings.

Consideration 2: What Are the Stakes Associated With the Results of the Site Visit?

Being clear about the stakes—both with the agency requesting the site visit and those at the visited program—is essential. Consider also the degree of standardization and transparency embedded within the site visit, especially when the stakes of the visit are high. Making the criteria for a positive rating clear and assuring interrater reliability among observers improves the perceived legitimacy of the site visit among grantees.

In the OFCY point-of-service quality site-visit example, the evaluation team elected to adopt a highly structured site-visit protocol that was shared in advance with staff of the visited program. This assured consistency across program sites and made the standards for success clearer to grantees. Moreover, site visitors were trained on the tool and demonstrated sufficient interrater reliability before going into the field. By contrast, although the site visit to the research center also carried high stakes, the singular nature of the center called for a more flexible approach that relied on a cadre of carefully selected content-area experts. When site visits are used to identify promising and innovative practices or to support continuous quality improvement— as in the research center site visit—it is appropriate to use a less-structured tool and to rely more on the observer's expert opinion.

Consideration 3: Will Sites Be Compared to One Another? In What Ways?

If site-visit results of multiple sites will be compared and contrasted in a systematic way, consideration of interrater reliability is paramount. Additionally, evaluators should use a structured site-visit tool—including indicators and a clearly defined measurement approach—and a common training protocol for site visitors. Evaluation teams should consider formal interrater reliability tests, such as having multiple visitors observe and rate the same program or activity. This differs from the more connoisseurship approach for evaluating a research center, which would not benefit from that kind of consistency. In compliance monitoring where comparisons may occur, such as Case One, a clearly defined process that supports dialogue between the evaluee and evaluator and a procedure that assures due process can be useful. This is important if self-assessment results vary considerably from the assessment of a well-trained evaluator.

NEW DIRECTIONS FOR EVALUATION • DOI: 10.1002/ev

Consideration 4: What Resources Are Available or Necessary for Analysis?

Site visits often yield volumes of qualitative data—planning in advance how to analyze and report it will help avoid unexpected timeline and budget challenges. For evaluation projects with limited time for qualitative analysis, using a structured site-visit tool that has preset scales and domains can speed the analysis process. There are instances in compliance-monitoring site visits and research center reviews when the visit is supplemented with quantitative data (e.g., student and enrollment data, earnings data, number of grants and publications) and evaluators need to understand the time lag inherent in that quantitative data. The site visit may shine a spotlight on best practices but the quantitative data may not yet reflect the impact of those practices simply because the data from big systems may lag behind practice by a year or more.

Consideration 5: What Considerations Are Necessary to Support Interpretation and Use?

Site visits have the potential to generate powerful, actionable information for the evaluee and the funder, because they can produce information that is both summative and formative in nature. It is valuable to both groups to have data for interpretation and use, but the use might be different depending on the audience. As such, evaluators must plan for use and give careful consideration to their role in creating user-friendly reporting tools and in supporting the evaluee's use of data to enhance organizational knowledge to improve practice or policy.

Conclusion

Site visits, whether incorporated into an evaluation design or as the evaluation in its entirety, can provide robust information to the evaluator, the funder, and the evaluee alike. Too often, site visits are poorly planned and executed or are not designed for a distinct and appropriate purpose. By taking the five considerations described in this chapter into account at the planning stage, evaluators can ensure that site visits are structured appropriately, yield useful information, and benefit the evaluator, the funder, and the evaluee.

References

Butler, L., & McAllister, I. (2011). Evaluating university research performance using metrics. *European Political Science, 10,* 44–58.

Eisner, E. W. (1998). *The enlightened eye: Qualitative inquiry and the enhancement of educational practice.* Upper Saddle River, NJ: Merrill.

General Accounting Office (GAO). (2003). *Program evaluation: An evaluation culture and collaborative partnerships help build agency capacity (GAO-03–454)*. Retrieved from http://www.gao.-gov/new.items/d03454.pdf

Lawrenz, F., Thao, M., & Johnson, K. (2012). Expert panel reviews of research centers: The site visit process. *Evaluation and Program Planning, 35*, 390–397.

Oakland Fund for Children and Youth. (2014). *Kids First! 2013–16 strategic investment plan*. Oakland, CA: Oakland Fund for Children and Youth.

Rons, N., DeBruyn, A., & Cornelis, J. (2011). Research evaluation per discipline: A peer review method and its outcomes. *Research Evaluation, 17*, 45–57.

Smith, C., Devaney, T., Akiva, T., & Sugar, S. (2009). Quality and accountability in the out-of-school-time sector. *New Directions for Youth Development, 121*, 109–127.

Yohalem, N., & Wilson-Ahlstrom, A. (with Fischer, S. & Shinn, M.). (2009, January). *Measuring youth program quality: A guide to assessment tools* (2nd ed.). Washington, DC: The Forum for Youth Investment. Retrieved from http://forumfyi.org/files/MeasuringYouth-ProgramQuality_2ndEd.pdf

COREY NEWHOUSE *is the founder and principal of Public Profit, an evaluation consultancy that helps mission-driven organizations measure and manage what matters.*

DENISE ROSELAND *earned her Ph.D. in evaluation studies from the University of Minnesota and is the founder/CEO of ChangeMaker Consulting, an independent consulting firm that works with nonprofits, government agencies, schools, and foundations to be more strategic and achieve greater impact.*

FRANCES LAWRENZ *is a professor in the Department of Educational Psychology with a specialization in STEM program evaluation and associate vice president for research for the University of Minnesota, Twin Cities.*

Capela, S., Frisino, J. M. (2017). Recipe for conducting quality accreditation site visits. In R. K. Nelson & D. L. Roseland (Eds.), *Conducting and Using Evaluative Site Visits. New Directions for Evaluation, 156*, 33–44.

3

Recipe for Conducting Quality Accreditation Site Visits

Stanley Capela, Joseph M. Frisino

Abstract

This chapter describes key ingredients that contribute to a successful accreditation site visit. The authors describe the site-visit process as it currently exists for organizations seeking accreditation from the Council on Accreditation (COA). The chapter focuses on the logistical aspects of a successful site visit rather than the results of the site visit itself. Based on their experience, the authors share key ingredients needed to ensure quality accreditation site visits. © 2017 Wiley Periodicals, Inc., and the American Evaluation Association.

This chapter describes key components of the Council on Accreditation's (COA) accreditation site-visit process, which we believe can serve as a reference and framework for a variety of types of site visits. COA's accreditation site-visit process was designed to evaluate the extent to which an organization has implemented COA's accreditation standards. During the site visit, a team of trained reviewers interview staff, board members, and other stakeholders; review organizational documents; conduct facility walkthroughs; and observe programs in operation. Organizations must meet between 350 and 1,000 standards, depending on the size of the organization and the number and types of its programs and services. Although most organizations seeking COA accreditation do so voluntarily, accreditation is increasingly being mandated by state regulatory and oversight entities. This means that an organization's ability to provide services may depend on whether it achieves and maintains its accreditation. For example, the North Carolina Department of Health and Human Services requires all licensed child-placing agencies to be accredited (Council on Accreditation, 2016b). This chapter describes the logistical aspects of a successful COA accreditation site visit rather than the results of the site visit itself. Based on our experience, we describe key ingredients of quality in accreditation site visits. We believe this detailed description of a highly structured and mature site-visit process can be instructive to evaluators who may want to adapt these processes to their own evaluative site visits.

Overview of the Council on Accreditation

COA is an independent, nonprofit accrediting body founded in 1977 by the Child Welfare League of America and Family Service America. According to the COA website, "COA accredits the full spectrum of child welfare, behavioral health, and community-based social services [and has] separate accreditation programs for private organization, public agencies, military family readiness programs, child and youth development programs, and international adoption programs" (Council on Accreditation, 2016a). COA accredits organizations for 4 years and the process takes 12–18 months to complete. COA standards address all aspects of an organization's administration, management, and service-delivery functions and accredits the entire organization and all its services. For example, an organization cannot choose to have its residential treatment programs accredited but not accredit its case management programs.

Components of COA Site-Visit Process

COA site visits can be described in terms of the typology presented in the first chapter of this volume. Typology dimensions are italicized. COA site visits are completely *standardized* and can have *high stakes*, because an organization's funding or continued existence may depend on becoming accredited. The *scope* includes the entire organization and all its programs and services, involving staff at every level from support staff to the Board of Directors. Site visitors receive 2 days of face-to-face *training* and must meet rigorous eligibility requirements. *Reporting* is highly structured and extensive, including ratings for hundreds of individual standards based on a four-level rating system with two passing levels and two not-passing levels. Finally, site visits are somewhat *collaborative*, because the visit schedule is developed with input from the review team leader and representatives of the organization under review. But with respect to methods, it is highly *externally directed*. All senior staff as well as the executive committee of the board and other board members must be available for interviews. A broad range of specific documents must be available for review, including a sample of client service records.

In the following section, we describe components of the COA site-visit process as it currently exists, which has changed very little over the 35 years since its development. As the service-delivery landscape evolves, COA standards and accreditation processes will necessarily evolve. The main components of the entire process include the self-study, pre–site-visit conference call, survey of stakeholders, selection of the review team, site visit, exit meeting, Pre-Commission Review Report, organizational response, post–site-visit surveys, and Commission review and decision making.

The Self-Study

COA's accreditation process typically takes 12–18 months to complete. The site visit is the most important milestone in the process, second only to the accreditation decision. During the site visit, a team of trained volunteer reviewers visits the organization's facilities to evaluate the extent to which it has met COA's accreditation standards. Leading up to the site visit, organizations undergo a lengthy and formal self-study process that typically takes 6–10 months to complete. During this period, they compare their practices against COA's standards, initiate new practices, or remediate self-identified deficiencies or gaps between current practices and the requirements of the standards. They also develop an evidentiary record that shows standards have been sufficiently implemented to justify earning accreditation. The formal self-study process ends approximately 6–8 weeks prior to the site visit. At the end of the self-study period, the organization submits a substantial number of documents to COA, which are collectively referred to as the organization's "self-study," which refers to both this collection of documents and the self-evaluation process.

One benefit of the self-study for the organizations is the opportunity to use COA's Performance and Quality Improvement standards to identify its strengths and challenges. The standards provide a way to design systems to best assess quality and to use data to identify and monitor a broad range of potential risks related to human resource management, contracting practices, financial risk, risks associated with use of restrictive behavior management practices, and use of treatment modalities. By doing the self-study and using the standards as a guide, the organization can set up a road map to design systems to address potential challenges and to identify the organization's strengths, which can be used to develop a brand that may positively influence potential funders.

Submission of the Self-Study

Submission of the organization's self-study is accomplished by uploading documents to a secure cloud-based portal. Once the self-study has been submitted, all members of the review team have access to the documents and begin reviewing them in preparation for the site visit. The introduction of this direct upload mechanism in 1996 has had a significant impact on this phase of the accreditation process. Although still time consuming for the organization, the upload process is significantly less time consuming than previous submission mechanisms. The previous system required the organization to copy all documents onto a CD or USB-drive and manually link these documents, which could number in the hundreds, within a mandatory COA-provided Excel spreadsheet. Prior to 1996, all self-studies were printed and a single organization's self-study could comprise thousands of pages organized in binders and filling multiple boxes.

The Review Team

COA reviewers are fact-finders for the Commission and do not decide if the organization is accredited. Accreditation decisions are made by the COA Accreditation Commission. This role distinction is an important safeguard against possible conflict of interest in the accreditation process and is discussed in more detail below. The role of reviewers is to examine evidence of completion against the requirements of each standard. Reviewers use their experience and professional judgment to assign a rating within the parameters of COA four-level rating system. Site review teams typically consist of one or two reviewers and a team leader.

Reviewer Qualifications

COA reviewers must meet rigorous eligibility criteria and undergo COA-sponsored training before being assigned to a review team to conduct an accreditation review. All COA reviewers are volunteers and receive no compensation. They volunteer to see how other organizations deliver services, to gain a deeper understanding of COA's accreditation process, to network with other professionals, and to contribute to making COA's accreditation process effective and affordable. Paying reviewers would significantly increase accreditation fees. Eligibility criteria include: employment at a COA-accredited organization; a graduate degree in a human service discipline or a non–human service degree; experience managing services provided to clients; at least 5 years of management experience; expertise in at least 5 of the more than 50 types of services that can be accredited by COA; and a letter of recommendation from an active COA volunteer, Accreditation Commissioner, or representative from one of COA's sponsoring or supporting organizations. When selecting reviewers for a team, the team leader matches the reviewer's knowledge, experience, and skills with the standards that will be addressed during the site visit to ensure the best available reviewer is conducting each review.

NEW DIRECTIONS FOR EVALUATION • DOI: 10.1002/ev

Reviewer Training

Once individuals meet COA's eligibility criteria they must undergo training. Formal training for reviewers and team leaders includes reviewer roles and responsibilities, methodology for rating standards, using professional judgment in the rating process, working as a team to develop consensus, and interviewing. Team leaders receive additional training in establishing a site-visit schedule, managing the team, and managing site-visit logistics.

Pre–Site-Visit Conference Call

The planning period between submission of the self-study documents and the site visit is very important to a successful site visit. A telephone call between the organization seeking accreditation and the review team leader occurs after the organization submits its self-study, usually at least 4 weeks prior to the site visit. There are several purposes to this call. It introduces the team leader and the organization's primary contact with COA to establish a sense of trust and rapport. The call also sets the site-visit schedule.

The call begins the process of establishing a schedule for the site visit, which may take several calls. The schedule must be established no later than 1 week prior to the site visit. This includes a schedule for formal interviews with key organization staff and the Board and a schedule of visits to service delivery sites. The schedule is established collaboratively between the team leader and the organization, but it can be changed once the site visit begins. The previsit conference call addresses logistics related to the review team's visit. These include travel to and from the site and travel by individual team members during the site visit between offices and service delivery sites, meals, and accommodations. The team leader uses the call to discuss any cultural dynamics within the organization that should be considered prior to the site visit. For example, some organizations may have a more casual dress code and others may require staff to wear business attire. This information helps the review team dress in accordance with the organization's prevailing norms.

The conference call also ensures the organization understands it must provide a private lockable room in which the review team can work while they are on site. The team leader and primary contact discuss details of the room setup, which requires that an internet-connected computer be placed inside the room. This is needed for confidentiality and to allow team members to leave their documents in a secure place when they leave to conduct interviews and visit other sites. Finally, the previsit conference call is the final opportunity to assess the organization's readiness for the site visit prior to its onset. COA can postpone or cancel a scheduled site visit if the team leader determines that the organization is not prepared.

NEW DIRECTIONS FOR EVALUATION • DOI: 10.1002/ev

Stakeholder Surveys

Structured surveys of organization stakeholders are an important source of evidence for COA's accreditation process. These mandatory internet or telephone surveys are administered to a sample of the organization's stakeholders and include questions about organization practices related to specific standards. Completing the surveys is voluntary for individual stakeholders and their names are not recorded unless they request a meeting with the review team while it is on site. Survey results are aggregated and go directly to the review team before the site visit. Surveyed stakeholders include board members, personnel, supervisors and managers, service recipients, representatives of similar community organizations and ones that are familiar with the work of the organization, and members of stakeholder advisory groups.

The Site Visit

COA's accreditation site visits typically consist of two or three reviewers who are on site conducting review activities over the course of 2 or 3 days. The number of team members and the number of days spent on site vary with the organization's size, number of service delivery program sites, or geographic distribution of sites. For larger organizations, the review team may visit a sample of program sites rather than visit every site. COA staff provides on-call support and consultation to the review team during site visits and on the weekend prior to the site visit when logistics snafus such as problems with lodging and transportation may occur. Review team support includes handling questions about how to interpret standards and questions about unique or unusual situations that were not identified prior to the site visit.

Sunday Document Review

Although the site visit officially begins on a Monday morning, the site visit usually begins on Sunday when the team arrives on site and reviews case records, personnel files, and other on-site documents. Team members will already be familiar with the organization, having read its self-study. The most important documents that will be reviewed are client case or service records. Case records are large and time-consuming to review, but more importantly, they provide a clear picture of service delivery.

Entrance Meeting

The site visit officially begins with a Monday morning entrance meeting during which the team leader talks to senior staff of the organization seeking accreditation. They discuss COA and the site-visit process in general, review the site-visit schedule, and answer any questions staff may have.

Interviews

The review team conducts formal and informal interviews with staff, governing body members, clients, and other stakeholders. Interviews with the chief executive, senior staff, the board chair, and program directors are conducted. There will also be formal interviews with staff and individual clients or groups of clients. Informal, unscheduled interviews with staff and stakeholders will also occur while the team is on site, particularly while visiting service-delivery sites. Informal interviews are more casual and take place in corridors, waiting areas, and other places where reviewers and stakeholders run into each other.

Visits to Service Delivery and Administrative Sites

Team members have scheduled visits to program sites and administrative offices and facilities to assess the degree to which current practices meet COA standards. Some of the specific things they observe include the safety, care, and maintenance of facilities and service-delivery sites with particular attention to residential facilities; programs in operation; interactions between staff and clients; and how client case records are maintained. They also conduct site-specific document reviews. When the team is unable to visit all service-delivery sites, the team informs the organizations of which sites will be visited a short time before the site visit starts. This short notification prevents organizations from preparing only those program sites that are on the site-visit schedule for a visit by the review team. Several factors may affect the decision but the team leader decides which specific sites will be visited. Team leaders may expand the number of sites they will visit beyond those in the initial schedule. Visits to program and administrative sites may also include observation of vehicles that transport clients, record storage and maintenance, and technological assets.

Daily Debrief

Toward the end of each day during the site visit, the team leader and the primary contact meet to discuss how the site visit is progressing. The conversation can include travel logistics, adjustments to the site-visit schedule for the next day, the need for additional data or documentation, and any other issues that warrant discussion.

Working Dinners

Individual team members operate independently after the entrance meeting, and it is common for team members to see very little of each other until the end of their working day. There is very little downtime once the site visit begins. Team members spend most of the day traveling to administrative offices and service-delivery sites, depending on which sections of standards they are assigned to review. The team meets for a working dinner at the end of each day, which is important, as team members may not have spoken to each other all day. The purpose of working dinners is to discuss overall impressions, areas of strength and concern, and to share information that other team members may need to rate their assigned standards. Working dinners help build team cohesion and the team leader uses working dinners to assess the strengths and competence of team members and provide guidance and mentoring.

Exit Meeting

The exit meeting is the formal conclusion of the site visit. The team leader will often meet with the organization's CEO prior to the exit meeting to provide an overview of the review team's findings. This is especially important if the team found areas of significant weakness that require substantial remediation to meet accreditation requirements. The formal exit meeting includes senior management, board members, and other key staff. It emphasizes the strengths observed during the visit and very generally covers challenges. Because the review team does not decide if an organization is accredited, ratings for specific standards are not discussed.

Precommission Review Report

After the exit meeting, the team leader submits the team's findings to COA where they are reviewed for consistency and thoroughness. COA sends a summary report of important findings to the organization. The report, called the Pre-Commission Review (PCR), only includes ratings for standards that must be remediated to allow accreditation. It does not include ratings for standards that the organization "passed" or ratings for standards that the organization "failed" but that by themselves would not prevent the organization from becoming accredited. The PCR is sent to the organization 2–3 weeks after the site visit. Ratings for all reviewed standards are provided once an accreditation decision has been made.

Remediation Period

Once the PCR is sent, the organization has 30–60 days to remediate any deficiencies that would prevent achieving accredited status. Approximately 70% of organizations require remediation following the site visit. Once the organization submits its response and any additional evidence required by the PCR, the Accreditation Commission reviews the review team's original report and the organization's response. The Accreditation Commission ultimately decides if the organization has sufficiently met the requirements to achieve the status as a COA-Accredited Organization. If COA determines the organization cannot be accredited, it can give the organization additional time to remediate deficiencies, deny accredited status, or suspend or put the organization on probation if it is pursuing reaccreditation.

Post–Site-Visit Surveys

After the site visit, COA sends organizations a survey asking about their experiences with the team and with individual reviewers. These surveys are an important source of information about reviewers in the field and the composition of review teams. Review team members are also surveyed after the site visit. They are asked to evaluate each other and their experiences with the site visit. This gives COA a continual stream of feedback about site-visit processes, applicability of specific standards, and performance of reviewers and team leaders.

Commission Review and Decision-Making

The Accreditation Commission is COA's decision-making body. They review the site-visit report and the organization's response to it and then render a decision as a group. Accreditation Commissioners are drawn from the pool of its most experienced team leaders and they too must meet eligibility criteria. They meet at least monthly to review organizations that have reached this final stage of the accreditation process. Until recently, the Commission reviewed all organizations anonymously to minimize or eliminate the possibility of bias or conflict of interest. In addition, Commissioners were required to recuse themselves if, during their review of the evidence, they become aware of the organization's identity and/or there is any other perceived or actual conflict of interest. This second safeguard is still in place, but a recent change in COA's database technology has made anonymous review impossible.

Safeguarding Quality in Accreditation Site Visits

In addition to the extensive training and eligibility requirements for reviewers and Commissioners, COA uses other safeguards to ensure the integrity of the site visit and accreditation decision-making (Frisino, 2002). Reviewers cannot review an organization that operates in the state or province in which the reviewer lives or works. This prohibition minimizes possible prejudice or favoritism that may result from competition for funding or other possible conflicts of interest. Reviewers cannot review an organization where they have previously been employed, served on its board, or if they know an employee or board member—unless the reviewer has not worked at the organization for more than 10 years and the executive leadership is no longer there. COA prohibits reviewers from advising organizations they are reviewing about how to meet the standards or otherwise consulting with them during and up to 1 year following the accreditation. Reviewers sign a confidentiality statement and agree to abide by a code of conduct, which clarifies COA's expectations of reviewers.

Organizational Factors Influencing Site-Visit Quality

When reviewing factors that contribute to a successful site visit, the most important is that the organization seeking accreditation has a CEO who fully supports the accreditation effort and can communicate the value of accreditation to staff and the board. Given the length of the accreditation process (an average of 17 months between application and decision) and the amount of staff and financial resources that must be invested, strong leadership is needed to keep the effort moving forward. A second factor that supports a successful site visit is the CEO appointing a person to lead the organization's accreditation effort who is organized and detail oriented, can work with staff at all levels of the organization, can organize staff, and can manage the process in a manner that encourages an organization-wide effort. Third, the organization has board leadership that is supportive of the process. COA's accreditation process requires the board to be an active part of the accreditation process. COA has numerous standards that address board functioning and for ensuring that the board meets its fiduciary responsibilities. Those responsibilities include oversight of the organization's financial management and risk management as well as responsibility for setting policy, long- and short-term planning, and resource development. A change in board culture and functioning may be required to become accredited. Fourth, the organization uses data from its quality-improvement process to improve program and client outcomes as well as monitoring management and operational performance. COA has rigorous quality improvement standards. Beyond the need to implement these standards, organizations can use their quality-improvement system to provide leaders with data on important standards, such as measuring progress toward achievement of strategic goals and objectives, risk prevention and management, and staff turnover. This in turn can give leaders a window on the organization's progress toward implementing key standards, particularly in areas that the organization knows will need improvement before accreditation can occur. Finally, there is motivation. Organizations seek accreditation for a variety of reasons. These can include the desire to achieve national recognition; funding requirements or funder incentives (e.g., state agency tiered reimbursement incentives); accreditation mandates, including consent decree compliance; and competitive positioning within the community. Or it may just be that a new CEO or the Board wants to challenge the organization and its staff to be more effective and efficient. Whatever the reason for seeking accreditation, an organization's motivation to achieve accredited status is a key factor in how seriously it approaches the self-study and the site visit. A motivated organization devotes the resources needed to conduct a rigorous self-study

NEW DIRECTIONS FOR EVALUATION • DOI: 10.1002/ev

and makes the changes in daily operations that may be necessary to become accredited.

Conclusion

We offer this overview of COA's accreditation site-visit process as an example of a comprehensive, multifaceted, structured process that has evolved over 35 years and has been applied tens of thousands of times. It has been used to evaluate organizations with as few as five staff and annual budgets under $100,000 to public agencies with as many as 10,000 staff and budgets exceeding $1 billion. COA site-visit processes were designed specifically to evaluate the extent to which an organization has implemented COA's accreditation standards. We would not expect COA's model to be adopted in whole for other related purposes. Nor are we suggesting that COA's is the best possible approach, or that it can or should be applied to other types of site visits, including to the site-visit processes of other accrediting bodies. We believe the COA site-visit framework can be broadly applied to different types of site visits. Accreditation is the culmination of a process that can take a year or more to complete and involve considerable investment of financial and staff resources. For some organizations mandated to become accredited, failure to do so can result in loss of funding or even going out of business. Even for organizations not under a mandate, a lot is riding on the site visit.

Whether or not the organization ultimately achieves accredited status, the authors strongly believe that the greatest benefit of the process is what is learned through the self-study–the in-depth self-evaluation that is at the core of the process. The self-study should result in a clear understanding of the organization's own strengths and challenges, which can foster a dialogue for improvement within the organization. Having a team of outsiders who will pass judgment on its efforts plays a major role in motivating the entire organization to stay focused and do the work necessary to demonstrate it has implemented the standards sufficiently to achieve accredited status. The process is intended to strengthen an organization's service-delivery system, make it more resilient, and reinforces the value the organization offers to meet the needs of the clients and the community it serves.

References

Council on Accreditation. (2016a). *About COA*. Retrieved from http://coanet.org/about/about-coa
Council on Accreditation. (2016b). *Recognitions*. Retrieved from http://coanet.org/accreditation/recognitions
Frisino, J. M. (2002). COA's accreditation system: Checks, balances, and firewalls. *Behavioral Health Accreditation and Accountability Alert, 7*, 4.

STANLEY CAPELA has conducted 106 site visits in 34 states, the District of Columbia, and Canada at for-profit, nonprofit, and 13 state and county agencies, as well as military site visits in the United States, Guam, Japan, and Germany.

JOE FRISINO has worked as a standards developer at the Council on Accreditation for more than 20 years.

NEW DIRECTIONS FOR EVALUATION • DOI: 10.1002/ev

Podems, D. R. (2017). Site visits: Necessary evil or garden of eden?. In R. K. Nelson & D. L. Roseland (Eds.), *Conducting and Using Evaluative Site Visits. New Directions for Evaluation*, 156, 45–55.

4

Site Visits: Necessary Evil or Garden of Eden?

Donna R. Podems

Abstract

In the evaluation literature, there is a dearth of guidance for conducting site visits. In 2015, Michael Patton aimed to fill that void by offering 10 standards for guiding site visits, and then invited others to contribute to this. This chapter accepts that invitation. By drawing on experiences gathered outside of the United States, the chapter suggests supplementing Patton's standards with four additional ones, namely, humor, honesty, humility, and humanity. © 2017 Wiley Periodicals, Inc., and the American Evaluation Association.

Setting the Scene

I live in South Africa and have conducted evaluation processes for nearly 25 years, 23 to be exact. Throughout, I have worked in over 25 countries in five different continents for more than 30 different donors and foundations. During this time, I have been a part of hundreds of site visits. I feel tired just writing that. These diverse experiences ground my understanding and, as such, I draw heavily on them. I engaged with other evaluators (who live and work outside of the United States) to further inform this chapter, and in doing so, I found compatriots whose experiences were equally, if not more, shocking, hilarious, sad, frustrating, and endearing than my own. During these conversations, I guided the discussion toward exploring the use of site visits, and what about them, if anything, made

them integral to an evaluation. It was within this wide spectrum that I selected three vignettes to illustrate diverse yet shared experiences.

In this chapter, it is an evaluator's perspective that I share, not the perspectives of those who are visited or those who commission them. Although
I recognize that these are important perspectives to hear, this chapter does
not bring that perspective. I acknowledge this limitation. Although these
other viewpoints would have likely provided a more holistic story, and perhaps deeper insight, I suggest that even one-sided stories bring value in the
experience, reflection, and subsequent lessons that they share, as long as
we remember: it is the evaluator's perspective.

This chapter grounds itself in Patton's draft standards for site visits,
posited in his book, *Qualitative Research and Evaluation Methods* (Patton,
2014) and later (Patton, 2015) in the *American Journal of Evaluation*.
Patton (2015) invited others to analyze their site-visit experiences, reach
their own conclusions, and share recommendations for improving the
practice. This chapter accepts that invitation and, drawing from vignettes
with not-so-unique sets of challenges, suggests supplementing Patton's
standards with four additional ones, namely, humor, honesty, humility, and
humanity. First, a bit on the term *site visit* and its interpretation.

Clarifying Concepts

Two concepts require clarification. One relates to how we label the act of
going into the field, and the other relates to the geography of the visit.

You Say Site Visit–I Say Field Visit

An evaluation site visit is when an evaluator or team of evaluators conduct
fieldwork in the place where the program, project, or intervention is taking
place, to observe what is happening independently (Patton, 2014, 2015).
Discussions with my colleagues revealed that we more often say "field visit"
and use this term to reflect the same purpose and action as a "site visit."
The evaluation field is known for multiple definitions of one word (e.g.,
evaluation, impact), so having two terms to describe one phenomena is not
surprising. The terms are used interchangeably in this chapter.

You Say Site Visit–I Say I Live Here

Locational perspective matters when discussing site visits. Living in South
Africa, I sometimes have confusing conversations with clients outside of
South Africa regarding the length of time and level of effort needed for a
site visit. In a recent evaluation, I had a team of South Africans, living in
Pretoria and Johannesburg, conducting an education evaluation in South
Africa. They spent two months in the cities in which they live conduct-
ing interviews at the different sites, with an additional month planned for
visiting schools in more rural areas. The donor knew that my team had

been visiting sites for 6 weeks in the cities in which they lived, thus it was perplexing when the donor continued to ask when my team was going to conduct site visits. Apparently, my United States donor only referred to site visits in reference to the rural schools, when my team needed travel. Therefore, it is likely that if my team had been North Americans, or Europeans, flown in to South Africa, the entire 3 months would have been considered a site visit. The confusion becomes an issue with planning, including level of effort, length of time in the field, and related budgeting, and in the final report, when communicating from where data emanate. In this chapter, I define a site visit as when an evaluator visits a place where an intervention is being implemented, even if it is in the evaluator's home town.

They Were the Best of Times

(*A Tale of Two Cities*, Charles Dickens, 1859)

As I start to write this chapter, the last conversation I had with a colleague about site visits still brings fits of giggles and tears of laughter to my eyes, all of which is making it very hard to write. As such, this story seems like a good start with which to ensnare a reader. It's a story about a site visit that took place in South Africa. But first, a little context is needed.

As part of my responsibility to give back, each year I donate approximately 80 hours of evaluation time to work in a nonprofit organization (NPO). This last year I spent my time with an organization for the blind where we identified some challenges with their job placement strategy and related interventions. We agreed that an evaluation could help to provide some insight and we worked together to focus questions and design a basic evaluation approach that included site visits. The organization contracted an evaluator to refine and implement the evaluation.

Using Patton's Standards

We drew on Patton's standards (2014, 2015) to guide the selection of the evaluator and to monitor her site-visit engagements. The evaluator met all 9 standards (although there are 10 standards, the final standard is follow-up and applies to the evaluation commissioner), which are presented systematically below.

Competence (1) and knowledge (2). She brought 10 years of experience implementing research and evaluations in multicultural settings. Her understanding of evaluative processes was built through years of conducting a range of evaluative processes using qualitative research in diverse settings from squatter camps to high-level government offices.

Preparation (3) and site-visit participation (4). In order to be well-prepared for the site visits, she spoke with the NPO's core team and read key documents, which informed what she needed to see and with whom she needed to speak.

Do no harm (5) and credible field work (6). Prior to the site visit, she engaged with people at each site to organize the visit, and through multiple emails and phone calls ensured that the purpose was clear. This aimed to quell any fear or stress felt by the people at the site. Further, she prepared thoughtful observation and interview guides informed by her literature and document reviews, and selected sites using explicit criteria.

Neutrality (7), debriefing (8), and site review (9). Conversations with the evaluator demonstrated that she was neutral, she debriefed the sites before she left, and she provided the report to those who responded that they wanted to see it.

Thus, she met all of Patton's standards for an effective site visit; she was professional, experienced, kind, well-prepared for each and every site visit, and thoughtful. You may be wondering, what's so funny? What I wrote here is true, but what I write below is truer, and where the laughter takes place and the learning begins.

The evaluator's first site visit to the organization's home office proved useful. She engaged with the intended users of the evaluation, interviewed the leadership, and familiarized herself with organization's culture. She was then well-prepared for her next site visit, which constituted a focus group with unemployed blind candidates who sought employment. She started the focus group by saying, "Hi, it's nice to see you." Silence. Then laughter. Hers and theirs. Thus, humor, though unintentional, and her ability to laugh at herself, laid the groundwork to establish rapport with the group. She recounts that she found the group easy to engage with, as they guided her through the interaction. One such example of this is when the evaluator asked the participants to indicate (by putting up their hands) who had sent out their CV in the last month. In the moment, the evaluator directed a question to one of the participants, by gesturing to him and saying "so in your experience...". When there was no response from the participant, she then rephrased the question, still directed at the one participant. Silence. She then realized that the group was starting to smile. One of the participants then said "you will need to be more specific, since we can't see who you are referring to." The evaluator, despite her meticulous preparation and careful thought about how to best engage during the site visit, realized there were just some things that she had to learn in the moment. This moment, in particular, made her aware of how often she relied on nonverbal communication and in this context, the need to use verbal ones.

Other site visits continued to toss new situations at her, such as meeting an expert on disability, who is a paraplegic. Upon entering the room, she offered to shake his hand despite her brain at the same time telling her not to do so. He laughed. She laughed. The site visit continued.

NEW DIRECTIONS FOR EVALUATION • DOI: 10.1002/ev

The Learning

These experiences demonstrate that no matter how prepared the evaluator is or how many years of experience is brought to bear, there will almost always be circumstances that are utterly and completely unpredictable, unexpected, and unforeseen. Hearing other similar (maybe not as funny) stories from experienced colleagues in other parts of the world, I asked them what guided them through these awkward moments. Two consistent themes emerged: humor and honesty. Humor—the self-deprecating kind. In other words, the ability to laugh at yourself. Need I say more? Honesty—acting with integrity, truthfulness, and straightforwardness. Admit your ignorance, inexperience, confusion, or uncertainty, and learn. If you are otherwise well-prepared, this does not make you a weak evaluator, rather it makes you a stronger one.

They Were (Still) the Best of Times

(*A Tale of Two Cities*, Charles Dickens, 1859)

In chatting with a Namibian colleague about her experiences with site visits, she reminded me of the indispensable roles that site visits played in a developmental evaluation we collaborated on some years back. She recounted how we used site visits to collect monitoring data from government departments, health clinics, and hospitals throughout the NPO's intervention, thereby providing the NPO will real-time data which they used to make informed decisions about the innovative intervention. This protracted time (a couple of days a month in the clinics, and 3 years in-country) at the sites grounded my evaluation team in the lived reality of the clinics, enabled the formation of relationships that deepened the level of data that they were able to obtain, provided insight needed to understand and analyze the data, and informed the focus of the final evaluation. But this is not the interesting story on which I want to focus, it is just the back story. The interesting part of the story comes next.

I detected a slight fervor in my colleague's voice as she reminisced about how site visits provided the evidence needed to triumph in our modernized version of the paradigm war. This is not the exhausted and virtually non-existent qualitative–quantitative one, but rather a related one that looks at those who believe site visits are necessary and those who do not. As the victor, it is our story that goes down in history. To keep the actors clear, my team is the evaluators and the other team is the researchers.

The Battle Scene

The donor required that the implementing NPO and my evaluation team collaborate with a research company. This research company brought a very

NEW DIRECTIONS FOR EVALUATION • DOI: 10.1002/ev

different worldview about program evaluation, which included eschewing field visits and qualitative data in general. The research team had a few focus points, one of which was to evaluate ambulance response time. This meant measuring the time it took for an ambulance to arrive at a health clinic to transport a critical patient to a hospital in response to a call from a Nursing Sister who was located at a health clinic. The NPO aimed to address this problem in several ways (the details are not relevant to this narrative) and the lead researcher assigned a Nursing Sister in each clinic to use their tool to record the ambulance response time in increments (e.g., 0–10 minutes, 11–20 minutes) and provide these data to the evaluation team's statistician, who sat in Europe. The research team did not visit any sites after their initial baseline study, proclaiming they had successfully used "similar tools that worked in other countries." Over time, the reported data, which were illustrated on a very fancy dashboard, showed that the ambulance response time had dropped considerably. While the research company decreed success and the donor cheered, my evaluation team and I silently called foul; it simply didn't resonate with our experiences at the clinics. However, at the time we had no empirical data with which to refute these findings.

Several months later, during a formative evaluation, I randomly placed my field workers at the different clinics to observe how the NPO's intervention had (or had not) improved the quality of service at the clinics. For example, sitting in a clinic all day, we observed the waiting times and patient experience (e.g., chairs provided, access to clean drinking water, engagement with nursing staff), access to condoms and relevant information, and the general atmosphere (e.g., welcoming when patients arrived, toilet paper and soap in the bathroom), all items that the NPO's intervention aimed to improve. The team interviewed patients who waited to see the Nursing Sister and inadvertently identified data when spouses or others, who accompanied the patient, offered to be interviewed. The site visits were physically draining on my team, yet I could not resist adding one more request. While at the sites, I asked my teams to observe anything to do with ambulances.

An observation at one site led to more focused observations at all sites, which led to more focused questions, which yielded data that explained the dashboard's identification of success. Here is how it happened. One of my evaluators observed what occurred when an ambulance was called but never arrived. She sent a text message to her evaluation colleagues about this observation and they in turn asked Nursing Sisters at their site about the ambulances and the recording of data. This led to more discussion with the Nursing Sisters at all sites and a deeper review of the dashboard data.

As a result of the nurses identifying the issue and explaining it to my team, we understood the following: rarely did the nurses write down exact response times, rather it was almost always a "guesstimate." Although this was a problem in terms of measurement; it didn't account for the trend of a lower response time. The Nursing Sister could just as easily be over-estimating the time. However, when a nurse called an ambulance and it did not arrive after a certain amount of time (the amount of time varied by site), the nurse marked the response time as "0–10" which was then averaged with other times and reported. When asked why this was marked, the nurses noted that "0" reflected no response; the chart did not have a "no response" column. When probed further, the nurses explained that these data were not useful to them. For instance, it did not improve their services to their patients and in their view, recording these data was an unnecessary extra task. Time recording was seen as an extra burden.

The site visit enabled the evaluation team to identify that the lower response time result did not reflect the success of the intervention. The site visit enabled direct observation, which led to an inquiry, where the experts (nurses) provided insight, which then produced data that led to useful contextualized findings about the lower recorded response times. Thus, the spoils of the battle (in this case the data) went to the victors (who we considered to be the NPO), who used this insight to inform decisions about their intervention and its measurement.

The Learning

The site-visit experience illustrates six lessons echoed by many of my colleagues. The first is the benefit of being able to observe what is happening physically and react to it, such as developing further questions, or identifying ways to gain additional observations. The second benefit is being able to engage with those who are the experts (in this case, the Nursing Sisters) to further understand what is being observed, and therefore gaining invaluable insight. A third point is the importance of being in the trenches surrounded by what you need to understand, which brings necessary contextual understanding. Fourth, observing, experiencing, or identifying what you did not even know that you needed to understand; fifth, gaining invaluable opportunities to listen to who needs to be heard; and sixth, to find others who otherwise may not have been heard, all of which provide precious data and insights. These six reasons suggest the vital role of site visits in an evaluative process and all six loosely fall under one theme, bringing the third addition to Patton's standards: humility. Although the evaluator brings a wealth of knowledge about evaluation, it is the people at the site who bring a wealth of knowledge about what is being evaluated. The evaluator is equal to others; not above or below them. This refutes an earlier claim by Lawrenz, Keiser, and Lavoie (2003), who claim that site visits rely heavily on the expertise of the visitors.

The next vignette describes a situation where the evaluator once again met all of Patton's nine standards, yet was presented with a set of challenges that were immitigable. It suggests the fourth addition to the site-visit standards, which is humanity.

They Were the Worst of Times

(*A Tale of Two Cities*, Charles Dickens, 1859)

Before the evaluation commenced, the donor's Board of Directors confirmed the evaluation's purpose and key evaluation questions. The team leader drew on this information to develop evaluation tools, which were tested and refined by local team members. With only 7 days in the field for site visits, the team spent months selecting sites and respondents, planning and confirming all interviews, and organizing logistics prior to the field visit. This resulted in a very focused, 7-day site-visit schedule, where our team planned to work in groups. Two international team members (myself and a Danish colleague), each traveling approximately 24 hours in economy class and passing through several time zones, arrived on a Sunday morning in an Asian country to join our three local team members, who resided in the country. Sunday afternoon included an intensive team discussion on the site-visit tools and review of logistics, followed by 7 days of site visits.

The Best-Laid Plans

On the first day, the team had planned—and re-confirmed prior to arriving in country—a meeting with the Board of Directors, who had requested this meeting to review the evaluation purpose and process. After the team waited for 2 hours, two of the eight Board Members arrived and demanded that the evaluation questions be changed. The Team Lead worked through the night to refocus the evaluation, change the field guides, and in the morning, update the team, all in time for the first site visit on the second day. On the second day, after the team waited for 2 hours outside the Program Director's door, the 2-hour confirmed interview was shifted to a 1-hour lunch in a noisy restaurant where it was difficult to hear and at a table so small it was even harder to write notes. On the third day, a critical interview was to take place with a key collaborating partner. After the evaluator drove for nearly 3 hours and arrived at the site, the partner apologized and rescheduled the meeting for the following morning. Now we needed to split the team on day 4 as other interviews were scheduled, so I attended this meeting alone. The meeting did take place; however, none of the five partner staff was familiar with the program, as they had simply been asked to "receive" the team. On the fifth day, the team took a 1-hour flight to the capital where interviews had been organized with various government departments. Upon arrival, the government departments, all of them, claimed that someone had cancelled these meetings, which had been re-confirmed the week prior by the local team members. It was not clear who cancelled them or why. One high-level official did agree to speak with the team. However, he refused to use a translator. His English was mostly unintelligible to the team, who sat and listened for over 90 minutes, not understanding much of what he said, and not gathering one piece of data. On the sixth day, the team visited a site where the local implementation team had planned a full agenda that included a lot of eating, walking, and one very, very long but not useful PowerPoint, which left little time for questions by the evaluation team. During the entire site visit, and for the remaining day, the team encountered similar and sometimes worse experiences, and therefore ended the site visit with few data to answer the evaluation questions and no second chances to gather more.

The Learning

Despite this dismal data collection (with regard to answering set evaluation questions), the site visit provided insight that the evaluation team would otherwise never have had. They learned that there was a dysfunctional board of directors and the possible challenges of collaborating with a partner whose staff overturned rapidly. They faced communication barriers in all forums, and weak relationships at the collaborative and management level, all of which appeared to influence the intervention negatively. In themselves, these are critical findings.

Unfortunately, in this example, the story doesn't have a funny or happy ending. The experience was belittled by the European consulting firm that contracted the evaluation team and the explanation of these site visits was seen as an excuse for a job poorly done. The findings that the team so desperately tried to communicate, which were core issues (e.g., dysfunctional board and strained relationships), were conveniently blocked and the Team Lead dismissed. These things happen.

Each colleague that I interviewed for this chapter related similar stories. When discussing these challenging experiences, there was one piece of advice that kept resurfacing—to remember one's humanity. A shortened definition of humanity is the quality or state of being human and showing kindness to other humans. We are human beings working with other human beings in socially complex and politically complicated, culturally situated, and sometimes stressful situations. Recognize and seek to understand how this may influence a visit, how it influences those visited, and how it affects those who assess the visit. It may change the site-visit experience or it may simply help one come to terms with it.

The Practicality of the Reality

I chose these vignettes to illustrate the wide variation of site-visit examples that I have encountered, which are echoed many times over by my colleagues. Site visits, when they are good, are very, very good. They support a worthwhile evaluation process that provides necessary data and contextual knowledge for the evaluation. When site visits are bad they can be very, very bad. I am not talking about the type of "bad" created by a rude, unprepared or otherwise culturally insensitive evaluator or one where the evaluator is tossed unwittingly into a situation beyond her control. Rather, I am referring to experiences similar to the one described in the chapter's final vignette. Yet, even at their very worst, site visits can provide contextual understanding used to further an evaluator's insight or identify useful critical findings that do not directly relate to the evaluation questions but can be used to strengthen an intervention—unless, of course, as described above, the evaluator is silenced.

The evaluator is not "off the hook," however when a site visit goes bad. When money is spent on a site visit that otherwise would have gone directly to the intervention (e.g., buying textbooks for children, providing inoculations for babies), it is an evaluator's responsibility to ensure that every realistic avenue is explored to warrant the expenditure of these resources. The avenue found for the negative experience described above is this chapter: being able to document the often hidden side of site visits, which can then be used to encourage a learning dialogue.

While I have focused on practical use, site visits have an intrinsic value, which is pinned on the belief that data interpretation will be flawed without understanding the context in which the intervention took place. An evaluator needs to bring together context and content to interpret data. Although different evaluation theorists would argue to what level that construction should (and can) take place (see Kushner, 1996; Stake, 1995; and Guba & Lincoln, 1994, who all bring different perspectives) the experiences shared by my colleagues combined with my own experiences posit that evaluation is inherently constructivist and suggests that site visits are an integral to part of this.

Conclusion

Site visits are an essential part of my work and that of my colleagues. Recognizing the reality that some things are beyond the evaluators' control is as important as knowing that others are planted firmly at their feet. With regards to the evaluator's role, I draw from anthropology and describe the evaluator's role as one that appreciates an etic (outsider) and emic (insider) perspective. The outside perspective provides the opportunity to identify what insiders may not see, while the evaluator aims to capture that insider perspective with which to understand and represent multiple perspectives from within that shared reality. The evaluator then draws on and intertwines these etic and emic experiences and perspectives to interpret the data (numbers and words), write the evaluation report, and, where required, provide recommendations. In an evaluation, data by themselves without contextual understanding are inadequate. However, the value of the site visit rests on various factors, many of which are identified in Patton's site-visit standards. Enhancing these with humor, honesty, humility, and humanity will increase the potential value of site visits. Although not exactly a contribution to

NEW DIRECTIONS FOR EVALUATION • DOI: 10.1002/ev

theory likely to be recognized by those living in the ivory tower, this chapter offers a contribution to those of us who exist in the field.

Thank you to Aimee White for her early in brainstorming on this article, and to the three thoughtful, reflective, and professional evaluation practitioners who allowed me to tell their stories. Some changes have been made to each narrative that ensure confidentiality yet do not alter the outcome.

References

Dickens, C. (1859). *A tale of two cities*. London, England: Chapman and Hall.

Guba, E. G., & Lincoln, Y. S. (1989). *Fourth generation evaluation*. London, England: Sage.

Kushner, S. (1996). The limits of constructivism in evaluation. *Evaluation, 2*, 189–200.

Lawrenz, F., Keiser, N., & Lavoie, B. (2003). Evaluative site visits: A methodological review. *American Journal of Evaluation, 24*, 341–352.

Patton, M. Q. (2014). *Qualitative research and evaluation*. Thousand Oaks, CA: Sage.

Patton, M. Q. (2015). Evaluation in the field: The need for site visit standards. *American Journal of Evaluation, 36*, 444–460.

Stake, R. E. (1995). *The art of case study research*. Retrieved from http://www.merriamwebster.com/dictionary/humanity

DONNA PODEMS *is a research associate at the University of Johannesburg and the founder and director of OtherWISE: Research and Evaluation, a small evaluation company in Cape Town, South Africa.*

Nelson, R. K. (2017). Stakeholder perspectives on site-visit quality and use. In R. K. Nelson & D. L. Roseland (Eds.), *Conducting and Using Evaluative Site Visits. New Directions for Evaluation, 156*, 57–73.

5

Stakeholder Perspectives on Site-Visit Quality and Use

Randi K. Nelson iD

Abstract

The chapter is an exploration of site-visit practices used in diverse program contexts based on individual telephone interviews in 2016 with 41 individuals who participated in site visits that were part of evaluations conducted within and outside of the United States. Participants included professional evaluators, site-visit commissioners, and staff of U.S. programs that were the subject of site visits. The findings are based on the diverse perspectives expressed about characteristics of effective site visitors, strategies for conducting high-quality site visits, and approaches to identifying and handling impression management. Most, but not all, participants said effective site visitors were those who had good interpersonal skills, content and evaluation expertise and knowledge, cultural competence, and were nonjudgmental. There were interesting differences of opinion among participants about the relative importance of content and evaluation expertise. Strategies for conducting effective site visits included careful preparation, having a clearly articulated and communicated purpose, focusing on learning and program improvement, setting a positive and collaborative tone, and using a team approach. Most participants said impression management on the part of program staff was common and not unexpected. Strategies to reduce the impact of impression management included triangulation of data sources, using elements of control and surprise in planning and conducting the visit, visiting frequently for longer periods, and focusing on learning and improvement. © 2017 Wiley Periodicals, Inc., and the American Evaluation Association.

Purpose

This chapter presents the views of a diverse group of evaluation stakeholders made up of evaluation practitioners, evaluation commissioners, and the staff of programs that are the subjects of evaluative and accreditation site visits. The study provides recommendations for conducting high-quality site visits based on their perspectives.

Methods

I recruited interviewees by purposive snowball sampling using my professional evaluation networks, including the American Evaluation Association (AEA) Local Affiliate Collaborative, the AEA Independent Consultants Topical Interest Group, the Minnesota Evaluation Association, and faculty and alumni of the University of Minnesota Evaluation Studies program. I invited people to participate in the study if they had conducted, commissioned, or hosted a site visit as a program coordinator or liaison. Interviewees received a list of interview topics before committing to an interview and were asked to recruit others who fit the selection criterion. I interviewed 41 people in telephone interviews during a 6-week period in 2016. Interviews lasted an average of 52 minutes and all but one was conducted as an individual interview. One was a group interview of two people who discussed the same program. Interview questions focused on (a) the rationales or purposes of site visits, (b) processes involved in commissioning and conducting site visits, (c) methods for ensuring high-quality site visits, and (d) strengths and limitations of site visits for evaluating programs. Table 5.1 lists the number and types of interviewees based on their role and if the evaluation was conducted in or outside of the United States.

Interviewees worked in a wide range of programmatic fields including K–12 and adult education, disability services, health care, organizational capacity building, tourism, poverty reduction, agriculture, and resource management. Programs were funded by private foundations, state and federal government agencies, and multilateral and bilateral donors. Six of the 41 people described experiences with accreditation site visits. Four people described the same program for adults in the criminal justice system, and two

Table 5.1. Role and Work Location of Interviewees

| Types of Interviewees | Number and Roles of People Interviewed | | |
	Total	United States	International
External evaluators	19	13	6
Internal evaluators	10	8	2
Commissioners	3	2	1
Program staff/liaisons	10	10	0
Total	41	33	9

described the same after-school program. Two of the 41 interviews were not included in the analysis because they were used primarily as guidance for modifying interview questions.

Analysis followed a rapid assessment protocol suggested by an interviewee (Neal, Neal, Van Dyke, & Kornbluh, 2015; Sobo, Simmes, & Landsverk, 2003). The method eliminates the costly and time-consuming step of transcribing audio recordings prior to analysis by coding directly from the audio recording. Based on this experience, it took 45 hours to analyze 31 hours of interviews. Analysis involved creating a preliminary codebook from listening to five interviews, replaying all interviews to tally responses in each person's codebook, adding codes to the codebook as necessary, and using transcription software to insert index marks in the audio recording to identify explanatory or illustrative comments. I transferred each person's tally marks to a master codebook spreadsheet to count responses, and aggregated responses by type of interviewee. The master codebook also contained verbatim or paraphrased comments inserted in spreadsheet cells. I modified the rapid analysis method by only counting a theme once per person regardless of the number of times that person commented on the theme. I exported all comments from cells in the spreadsheet to a Word document with the use of a Visual Basic program downloaded from the Internet (https://www.extendoffice.com/documents/excel/1579-excel-export-comments-to-word.html), to organize and analyze comments by theme and speaker. I reviewed all comments for each theme and regrouped or condensed themes as needed. The percentages listed in Tables 5.2–5.5 are calculated based on the number of interviewees whose responses were coded to a theme divided by the number of interviewees in the group. Verbatim and paraphrased comments from interviewees were included to clarify the meaning of themes and highlight variations within and among groups. The responses of the two commissioners are included in the narrative but not tables, because including them in frequency calculations would have inflated their contribution.

Findings

Several topics were included in the interviews but were excluded from the findings because of chapter-length limits. These include purposes and stakes of site visits; added value of site visits; opportunities for site feedback; reporting; the costs, strengths, limitations of site visits; and the impact of anticipation of site visits. Therefore, this chapter focuses on strategies and approaches to improve the quality of site visits and includes (a) characteristics of effective site visitors, (b) strategies for conducting high-quality site visits, and (c) identifying and handling impression management. Unless noted, the themes included in Tables 5.2–5.5 are ones that were discussed by at least half of the evaluator or program staff subgroups. Data were disaggregated by role in the evaluation, which resulted in very small samples in some cases. This limitation of the study should be considered when making inferences from these data.

Characteristics of Effective Site Visitors

Table 5.2 includes themes related to the skills or qualities of effective site visitors. It is interesting to note the differences of opinions between international and U.S. evaluators about the need for content and evaluation expertise or knowledge, which is discussed in detail in the following section. The four characteristics of effective site visitors mentioned most frequently by all evaluators combined were interpersonal skills, mentioned by 59% of all evaluators, followed by content expertise (48%), content knowledge (44%), and an evaluation team having complementary skills (44%). Site visitors being nonjudgmental was mentioned by 50% of program staff (Table 5.2).

Interpersonal Skills

Interviewees highlighted the importance of interpersonal skills for conducting an effective site visit. These included having the ability to make people comfortable, being approachable and friendly, communicating diplomatically, and acting with humility and respect. People described respect as being aware of and appreciating the time program staff and participants were giving to participate in the site visit. Some described interpersonal skills in terms of being "personable and compassionate" whereas others emphasized the need for site visitors to be "nonjudgmental"—letting site staff know the evaluator is interested in learning about their program

Table 5.2. Skills and Qualities of Effective Site Visitors

	Percentage of Each Group Who Referenced the Theme				
Qualities of a Good Site Visitor	All Evaluators N = 27	U.S.[a] N = 13	Intl[b] N = 6	IE[c] N = 8	PS[d] N = 10
Interpersonal skills	59	62	67	50	60
Content expertise	48	38	67	50	80
Content knowledge	44	62	17	38	30
Team-complementary skills	44	54	50	25	10
Evaluation expertise	37	23	67	38	10
Evaluation knowledge	37	62	17	13	20
Cultural competence	26	8	67	25	20
Nonjudgmental	19	15	17	25	50

[a]U.S. evaluators.
[b]International evaluators.
[c]Internal evaluators.
[d]Program staff.

NEW DIRECTIONS FOR EVALUATION • DOI: 10.1002/ev

rather than catching them making mistakes. An evaluator working outside of the United States recommended a site visitor should "not act like a police officer" and a U.S. evaluator said a site visitor should not "wear the expert badge." Other interpersonal skills interviewees included in this theme were flexibility and the ability to work effectively on a team. One commissioner said interpersonal skills were important.

Content Expertise and Knowledge

People said content expertise allowed evaluators to ask better questions. Program staff said they did not want to have to "waste time" educating uninformed evaluators about program activities, the systems in which they did their work, or technical terminology. Many program staff wanted site visitors to be content experts and leaders in their field so they could provide professional consultation, share best practices, and connect staff with others in the field doing similar work. Neither commissioner said content expertise was required and one voiced a concern that content expertise could lead to having "such strong opinions that (it) influences their evaluation."

Interviewees who said site visitors should be knowledgeable about content—but not necessarily experts—highlighted the novel perspectives these site visitors brought to bear on programs and issues. An evaluator said, "novices can see some interesting things since [they] have fewer preconceptions about issues [and] programs." Others thought evaluators without content expertise could teach themselves about content on the job and through research. Program staff expected site visitors to "be knowledgeable about us and the community we serve."

Evaluation Expertise and Knowledge

There were also differences of opinion about evaluation expertise and knowledge. Although almost half (48%) of all respondents said content expertise was important, there was a large range in frequencies of responses among groups (Table 5.2). A high proportion of U.S. evaluators said content knowledge was important (62%), but only 38% said content expertise was needed. The situation was reversed for international evaluators, with 67% saying content expertise was needed and only 17% saying content knowledge was important. Almost all program staff (80%) said content expertise was necessary when evaluating complex and specialized programs.

Among those who said site visitors should have evaluation expertise, defined it as having an advanced degree or extensive coursework in evaluation generally and in qualitative methods, specifically. Others described expertise as being trained in using highly structured observation tools or accreditation standards and being skilled in research design and statistics. An internal evaluator described desirable evaluation expertise as having "broad knowledge of program and policy evaluation and an analytical mind to systematically and logically address evaluation and data."

Interviewees described other desirable evaluation skills, such as managing and interpreting data and project management; being "able to assimilate lots of new information-data quickly, [which is] especially important if the visitor is not a content expert"; and being a "pattern-finder" who can distill the big picture from the details. One evaluator said an evaluator could be adept in qualitative data collection without being an evaluation expert but that without expertise, they would likely "have difficulty synthesizing qualitative and quantitative data" well enough to tell the "full story." The two commissioners split on their views of the relative importance of evaluation expertise and knowledge.

Cultural Competence

Relatively few evaluators (26%) discussed cultural competence as an important characteristic of an effective site visitor (Table 5.2). However, frequencies of responses about cultural competence ranged widely from 8% for U.S. evaluators to 67% for international evaluators. Those working in international settings said it was important to work in teams of people with complementary skills that included knowledge of local conditions, cultures, and languages. International evaluators focused more on understanding local written and spoken languages as elements of cultural competence and U.S. evaluators emphasized understanding the communities served. Other interviewees also identified cultural competence as a specific and essential skill of an effective site visitor. An internal evaluator said cultural competence "was too often lacking [and evaluators] need to be aware of (their) own biases about the population being served." Another commented on the need to "make the voices of participants heard and reflected in the report." An evaluator who had a particularly bad experience recounted how a site visitor's racist and sexist jokes offended everyone on site and interfered with the evaluation. One of the two evaluation commissioners described cultural competence as an important attribute of site visitors.

Nonjudgmental

Being nonjudgmental was mentioned by only 19% of all evaluators but by 50% of the program staff (Table 5.2). Evaluators described the need to be curious and interested in learning, of going "beyond delivering bad news to help people improve." An external evaluator said you need to be able to observe without judgment, because it interferes with your ability to observe effectively. Internal evaluators said it was important to "not act like a judge but instead act as a partner." Program staff said site visitors should "be open-minded about the project," to not approach the process "as a formality but instead [be someone who] wants your program to improve and be successful." A program staff person who took part in an accreditation site visit suggested that evaluators come into the visit "unarmed [with a] kinder and gentler approach that makes it easier for site staff to talk frankly."

NEW DIRECTIONS FOR EVALUATION • DOI: 10.1002/ev

Although there is overlap between this theme and the theme of interpersonal skills and the purpose of site visits, it is worth noting that evaluators and site staff alike appreciated a nonjudgmental and learning approach to site visits. Neither commissioner discussed this theme.

Strategies for Conducting Effective Site Visits

Table 5.3 summarizes the themes derived from interviewees' comments about what good site visits look like and how people should conduct effective site visits. Themes are grouped into four main categories: preparation, purpose, tone, and using a team approach.

Preparation

Evaluators and program staff alike noted the importance of preparing for a site visit well in advance of the actual visit. Preparation included planning for the logistics of the visit, giving notice of upcoming visits, developing protocols and agendas, and doing one's "homework" to learn as much as possible about the program and context before arriving on site.

Plan the visit. There was a wide range in the number of people who discussed the importance of planning. Although slightly more than half of all evaluators (56%) said it was important, relatively few internal evaluators (38%) and 83% of international evaluators identified planning as an

Table 5.3. Strategies for Effective Site Visits

| Site-Visit Characteristics | Percentage of Each Group Who Referenced the Theme | | | | |
	All Evaluators $N = 27$	U.S.[a] $N = 13$	Intl[b] $N = 6$	IE[c] $N = 8$	PS[d] $N = 10$
Preparation					
Plan the visit	56	54	83	38	50
Give notice	48	62	17	50	60
Develop protocols	44	62	33	25	10
Do your "homework"	30	31	50	13	30
Purpose					
Communicate the purpose	48	62	17	50	10
Aligned to phase, questions	44	62	17	38	0
Focus on learning	33	31	33	38	50
Tone					
Collegial	41	31	50	50	50
Flexible	37	38	50	25	40
Team of visitors	41	54	50	13	20

[a]U.S. evaluators.
[b]International evaluators.
[c]Internal evaluators.
[d]Program staff.

important strategy for conducting an effective site visit (Table 5.3). Evaluators said it was important to account for logistics and local schedules to use their limited time on site efficiently. Logistics included things as pragmatic as knowing "where to park and what door to enter" at a school and knowing the school's guidelines and rules about visiting classrooms. Preparation was especially important for evaluators working far from home, because leaving a site to return at a more convenient time was usually not an option. An international evaluator emphasized the importance of considering local holidays and seasons to optimize gaining access to sites and program stakeholders. A commissioner said planning was important so the evaluator could meet "all of the critical partners and players" to see the same issue from multiple perspectives.

Give notice. Developing and providing program sites with an agenda that includes the "who, what, when, where, why, and how" of an upcoming visit was an important aspect of planning. There were interesting variations in numbers of interviewees who said it was important to give prior notice of upcoming visits. Only 17% of international evaluators said this was important for conducting effective site visits (Table 5.3). The groups that mentioned this most often were U.S. evaluators (62%) and program staff (60%). Evaluators described the need to be "transparent" to reduce program stakeholders' fears about what would happen during a site visit and to keep them from feeling "ambushed." International evaluators said it was often too difficult to get to remote sites without providing notice to the program site liaisons in advance of the visit. Program staff appreciated getting notified in advance so they could "be prepared and have the right people on hand" to answer the evaluators' questions efficiently and not waste the time of interviewees. However, one site coordinator said it was also important for evaluators to be able to "drop in" on a program without notice in cases where fraud was suspected. Program staff involved in accreditation site visits had the advantage of knowing the kinds of issues they would need to address during a site visit, because the issues had already been reported in their self-study. Both commissioners commented on the importance of evaluators providing notice in advance of the visit and communicating with funders and program staff throughout site-visit planning and implementation.

Develop protocols. Preparing data collection protocols and tools and training team members in their use were other important aspects of planning. A high proportion of U.S. evaluators (62%) commented on the need to develop protocols, but only 33% of international evaluators mentioned it (Table 5.3). A U.S. evaluator said interview protocols should be semistructured so evaluators could add questions or probe as needed during the site visit. However, the same evaluator said observation tools should be standardized for consistency across sites. An internal evaluator highlighted the value of using a nationally recognized observation protocol to ensure applying the same definitions of quality. International evaluators said

New Directions for Evaluation • DOI: 10.1002/ev

data-collection instruments should be developed before arriving in the field but that piloting and revising instruments had to occur to adapt them to local conditions. One of the two commissioners said preparing agendas in advance of the site visit was important.

Do your homework. Evaluators said learning as much as possible about the program in advance of the visit was an essential part of planning. Half of the international evaluators said this was important to conducting an effective site visit and fewer U.S. (31%) and internal evaluators (13%) discussed the importance of this aspect of preparation (Table 5.3). Doing one's homework allowed evaluators to "know enough about the program to ask the right questions." Planning allowed program staff liaisons to coordinate schedules of staff and recruit relevant stakeholders for interviews. An internal international evaluator noted the importance of careful scheduling so expensive "experts aren't tied up in the field for the whole visit if [they] are only needed for part of one of the days." In domestic evaluative site visits, evaluators were only present for 1 or 2 days, although accreditation visits typically took 5 days and international external evaluation site visits lasted several weeks. With condensed visit schedules, planning was crucial to use everyone's time efficiently and to gather all data needed to answer evaluation questions fully.

Clarity of Purpose

Being clear about the purpose of the site visit was described by 33%–48% of all the evaluators interviewed for the project (Table 5.3). Related ideas include communicating the purpose of the evaluation and site visit to stakeholders, aligning the site-visit procedures to the phase of the program and the evaluation questions, and focusing the evaluation on learning and program improvement.

Establish and communicate the purpose. Almost half of all evaluators (48%) but relatively few program staff (10%) said it was important to communicate the purpose of the site visit in advance (Table 5.3). More U.S. than international evaluators discussed the importance of communicating the site visit's purpose (62% and 17%, respectively). An international evaluator said, "in some countries, evaluation is not a well-known concept [so] they think of it as an audit—make sure they know this is not an audit to put their minds at ease." Internal evaluators said it was important to be clear if the purpose of the site visit was to improve quality of services rather than to defund or terminate a program. One internal evaluator began the site visit with a kickoff meeting for all stakeholders to clarify the purpose and set the tone for the site visit. A program staff liaison said it was important that everyone—including the evaluators—understand if the site visit is "a box-checking site visit or an improvement-focused site visit."

Align to purpose and phase. Many U.S. evaluators (62%) said aligning the site visit to the purpose of the evaluation and the phase of the

NEW DIRECTIONS FOR EVALUATION • DOI: 10.1002/ev

program or grant cycle influenced the usefulness of the site visit (Table 5.3). Many said it was important be "selective" in deciding to conduct a site visit, that one should "only do a site visit if it is what you need to do to answer the evaluation questions . . . and if it adds richness to your data." They said it was important to avoid including a site visit by default by making sure a site visit was necessary and likely to add important information. Some suggested delaying site visits until programs were "settled" or ready to be evaluated. Others recommended conducting site visits early to midpoint in the program or grant cycle to catch problems early enough to fix them.

Focus on learning. More program staff than evaluators said a site visit should focus on learning and program improvement (50% and 33%, respectively, Table 5.3). Evaluators said it was important to highlight program successes and to learn about what worked, to help organizations reach their goals, and to help programs improve. An internal evaluator said it was important to "get away from a checklist approach to engage and appeal to common goals, [to show] funders and grantees are partners for meeting a common goal." Another internal evaluator said evaluators must "focus on [the program's] action plan for improvement, not their quality scores." A program staff person described a learning focus as one where "we can ask questions of the experts that are doing the site visit . . . like a consultation, a chance to connect with other organizations." One of the two commissioners said it was important the site visit had a learning and improvement focus.

Establish the Tone

Based on the comments of evaluators and program staff alike, the tone set by the evaluator has an important influence on the quality of the site visit. Tone included establishing a collegial, collaborative, and respectful atmosphere and taking a flexible approach to the visit to limit disrupting program operations.

Collegial tone. Half of the international evaluators, internal evaluators, and program staff said setting a collegial tone was important to conducting an effective site visit (Table 5.3). Fewer U.S. evaluators said a collegial tone was important (31%).

An international evaluator described the necessity of establishing a collegial and respectful tone with program staff by saying:

> A lot has to do with the attitude that you bring. It makes a difference in how they respond and how open they are in terms of sharing information and cooperating. I see the beneficiaries and stakeholders as the local experts. They know the program—their slice of it—better than anybody else because they live it day in and day out; we are just parachuting in for a couple of weeks . . . . I try to come with that attitude that if you are a poor farmer here you are an expert essentially. Having a spirit of inquiry that we are all in this together to try to learn together—you can make it a positive experience.

Internal evaluators also commented on the need to be collegial with program stakeholders to create a partnership to achieve common goals rather than taking the role of the "judge or auditor." Another internal evaluator said it was important for the evaluator to interact with program participants rather than to observe them as if they were specimens in "a zoo," to learn from program staff rather than sitting back as an expert to judge the program and people. A program staff person expressed collegiality in different terms by saying:

> If we have some say in scheduling, that makes a big difference [there is a] restorative justice principle—are you doing things for people, to people, against people or with people? So, if they are doing it *to* us as opposed to *with* us—to be able to say, "we would like to schedule a visit to come out, let's schedule something next quarter"—that gives us a lot more latitude . . . so it can feel really oppressive and scary or it can feel really collegial and supportive.

For evaluators and program staff alike, having a collegial relationship meant showing respect for each other, which was expressed by using time well, avoiding disrupting program staff in their work as much as possible, and being respectful of local context and customs. A program staff person involved in accreditation visits commented on the need for mutual respect and courtesy by saying evaluators should treat the staff with "kindness and gentleness" and the site should act like a "good host" for the evaluators. One commissioner said it was important that evaluators set a partnership tone and respect the time staff needed to do their work while still participating in the evaluation.

Flexibility. The only interview question that elicited laughter from evaluators was about adapting site-visit protocols upon arrival in the field "since nothing goes exactly as planned." Half of the international evaluators, 40% of the program staff, and 38% of U.S. evaluators commented on the importance of remaining flexible when conducting effective site visits (Table 5.3). Only 25% of internal evaluators commented on this aspect of site-visit tone. All evaluators said they created detailed agendas prior to arriving on site, but they also recognized the need for flexible planning to adapt to local conditions—to be "fluid within the plan" and to "stick to the agenda but be flexible to accommodate availability of interviewees." Changing local conditions that required flexibility included sickness of key informants or their children, floods, blizzards, and emergency meetings of key informants. A program liaison said it was important that evaluators were mentally nimble enough to see new things and ask new questions, rather than be limited to items on a checklist of interview questions or things to observe. One evaluator said humility was important and necessary to recognize program staff's time was important and to be willing to wait or reschedule your own plans to accommodate theirs. A commissioner expressed the view it was important to "be more adaptive—not so hardcore with the agenda or questions ... so you can be nimble enough to adapt to situations that come up."

Changing the site-visit protocol, while still meeting the objectives of the evaluation, was sometimes challenging but necessary. For example, a site coordinator used her knowledge of local conditions to influence the evaluator to conduct individual interviews instead of focus groups because of logistical problems associated with doing group interviews in a prison setting. An international evaluator adapted his field data collection protocol by substituting a focus group for a household survey when he found a recent household survey had recently been completed in the community. In some cases, changing the protocol can be very difficult and incur delays in data collection. An evaluator gave an example of having to resubmit a data collection instrument for Institutional Review Board approval because the protocol had to be changed to adapt to field conditions. A site liaison noted it is "difficult to make changes to the protocol when many enumerators [are] evaluating many different sites" spread across the country. Federally funded programs were described as more detailed and rigid in scope and agendas than those funded by foundations, but there appeared to be a great deal of variation among funders.

Work in a Team

Evaluators suggested using teams of site visitors to manage logistics, provide multiple perspectives, and take advantage of complementary skills. Half of international evaluators and 54% of U.S. evaluators said a team approach improved the effectiveness of site visits (Table 5.3). Only 13% of internal evaluators and 20% of staff identified using teams of evaluators to improve site visits. An evaluation commissioner said logistics were managed more easily when one person was available to take notes and the other to facilitate conversations. Other interviewees said having a team of people with different discipline expertise and experience provided "a different lens" for interpreting data. They noted that it was important that the team had trained together and had been involved in planning from the beginning rather than being pulled together only for field data collection. For evaluators operating internationally, it was important to include someone on the team who knew local languages and cultural issues. In situations where a representative of the project or funder accompanied the evaluators during a site visit, one evaluator found it helpful for one team member to engage them so the other evaluator could talk more openly with program staff or beneficiaries. In almost all cases where people discussed a team approach, they said it was important to include people who had content and evaluation expertise and who could work together effectively as a team.

Table 5.4. Incidence of Impression Management

| | Percentage of Each Group Who Referenced the Theme | | | | |
| | All Evaluators N = 27 | U.S.[a] N = 13 | Intl[b] N = 6 | IE[c] N = 8 | PS[d] N = 10 |
Prevalence					
Happens	89	92	100	75	70
Does not happen	22	31	17	13	20

[a]U.S. evaluators.
[b]International evaluators.
[c]Internal evaluators.
[d]Program staff.

Identifying and Handling Impression Management

Impression management is the attempt to manage or influence how other people view you or your organization (Norris, 2011). In most cases people attempt to show their programs in the most positive light possible. However, some program stakeholders may highlight the negatives to force funders to take notice and increase funding or extend the program to solve the highlighted problems. During interviews conducted for this study, people were asked if they thought positive impression management took place during site visits and, if so, how its impact could be mitigated (Table 5.4).

Impression Management Happens

A high proportion of all evaluators (89%), 75% of internal evaluators, and 70% of program staff said they thought impression management occurred during site visits. All international evaluators and 92% of U.S. evaluators shared the same view. External U.S. evaluators described impression management as an expected and natural human response that was not unique to site visits. A few said upper managers were more likely to attempt to manage impressions than were line staff, especially if funding was perceived to be at stake. An international evaluator described the situation by saying "they are trying to give you the best picture, that everything is great, perfect, no problems." Another said people want to improve their programs but they also have strong incentives to make them sound very positive. One of the two commissioners said they thought impression management occurred.

A few interviewees said impression management was a good thing because it resulted in staff showing their programs at their best and they would worry if program staff were not doing their best during a site visit. An internal evaluator described wanting people to be running the program as well as possible because they were evaluating how the intervention worked when it was being implemented properly. Two program staff said the

NEW DIRECTIONS FOR EVALUATION • DOI: 10.1002/ev

accreditation body expected programs to show their best work and present their organizations in the best light.

Impression Management Does Not Happen

Only 22% of all evaluators and 20% of program staff said they thought impression management did *not* occur during site visits (Table 5.4). Some said it did not occur because site coordinators lacked the power to influence the behavior of staff or other stakeholders or that program staff had such intense work that they did not have the time or energy to sustain a "show" over time. An internal evaluator working internationally said program stakeholders were more open to sharing problems during a monitoring and evaluation visit than during a technical audit conducted by external evaluators. A site coordinator said it made no sense to cover up problems, because by doing so they would forfeit expert advice from site visitors who could help them improve the program. One of the two commissioners said they did not think impression management occurred because they had heard "quite critical things" about the program from site-visit findings. The same person said they thought impression management happened more often with phone interviews than site visits.

Detecting and Mitigating Impression Management

Interviewees offered suggestions for reducing the impact of impression management on the quality of the site-visit and its findings. Table 5.5 summarizes the themes from comments made by at least 30% of the interviewee groups, because very few strategies were common to 50% of any group. Strategies to mitigate impression management included triangulation, use of control or surprise, visit frequency and duration, and having a learning or improvement focus.

Table 5.5. Strategies to Reduce the Impact of Impression Management

	Percentage of Each Group Who Referenced the Theme				
Mitigation Strategies	All Evaluators N = 27	U.S.[a] N = 13	Intl[b] N = 6	IE[c] N = 8	PS[d] N = 10
Triangulation	67	77	67	50	50
Control and surprise	59	54	83	50	10
Visit frequency and duration	30	38	33	13	0
Learning and improvement focus	30	31	33	25	20

[a]U.S. evaluators.
[b]International evaluators.
[c]Internal evaluators.
[d]Program staff.

NEW DIRECTIONS FOR EVALUATION • DOI: 10.1002/ev

Triangulation. Evaluators described triangulation in the sense of interviewing diverse stakeholder groups, those within the program as well as external stakeholders who have less incentive to "embellish the truth." Sixty-seven percent of all evaluators suggested using triangulation as a strategy to mitigate impression management (Table 5.5). Only 50% of internal evaluators and program staff mentioned triangulation as a strategy. An evaluator described the importance of interviewing people at all levels within the program's organization because "sooner or later, someone spills the dirt." Several stressed the importance of interviewing program clients or beneficiaries individually and in groups in the absence of program staff to get their unfiltered views of the program. Evaluators who worked with youth-serving organizations appreciated the tendency of children and youth to speak up when staff deviated from normal behaviors or activities. Others described a process of corroborating data by asking people about issues raised earlier by others at the same site or at different sites. Several evaluators described triangulation as checking the consistency of data between what you see and hear on site and the reports or self-studies filed before the visit. A commissioner said impression management was easier to detect in focus groups, because focus-group participants' reactions often gave away the perpetrator.

Control and surprise. Evaluators differed in their views of sharing or keeping control of the site visit and using the element of surprise to reduce impression management. Of the 59% of all evaluators who commented on control and surprise (Table 5.5), 7% commented on using surprise and 22% commented on control. Among all evaluators who commented on the element of surprise, 7% said the visit should not be like a "pop quiz" and 11% said it should be. A few (19%) said some but not all aspects of the visit should be a surprise and that a middle ground was possible, such as by conducting "serendipitous observation" of off-tour events and places and "keeping your eyes open" when in the field.

Evaluators recognized the limits on their own control over the site visit and their need to share control with program liaisons. Of the 22% who commented on the aspect of control, 7% said the evaluator should keep control of the visit and 15% said control should be shared with program staff or the client. Several said they would prefer to select sites and people randomly, but they recognized this was usually not feasible considering transportation issues in getting to the field or coordinating schedules of staff for interviews during the short period of the visit. An international evaluator said it was important to visit sites "they are not pushing you to see" or make a point of visiting successful sites in addition to those that are struggling. A commissioner said it was important to leave funders at home to balance power dynamics during a site visit.

Visit frequency and duration. Almost one-third of all evaluators (30%) said more frequent and longer site visits fostered more effective long-term engagement and allowed the evaluator to become "part of the routine" or "community," which reduced the incidence and impact of impression management (Table 5.5). More U.S. and international evaluators (38% and 33%) shared this view than did internal evaluators (13%). None of the program staff commented on visit frequency or duration. One evaluator described being able to "see the cracks" when visits lasted longer. Evaluators recognized the increased cost of doing multiple visits but said it was preferable to do multiple visits of fewer sites rather than only one visit per site. One commissioner commented on the need for more frequent and longer site visits.

Learning and improvement focus. Almost one-third (30%) of all evaluators said conducting site visits with a learning or improvement focus mitigated impression management (Table 5.5). They said there was less incentive for program staff to present an overly positive view of the program when the focus of the site visit was learning and program improvement. Other evaluators emphasized the importance of seeing things as they are so funders would know how to improve program quality or provide technical assistance. An internal evaluator said it was important to make it clear to grantees that they would not be penalized if they came to the funder to ask for help if they were having problems. Commissioners said it was important to hear both the positive and negative things about a program and evaluators need to make the site visit "a safe place to be honest" with others to support "learning from mistakes."

Conclusion

I was inspired to end this chapter with questions because of the Director of the National Institute of Justice's 2012 Director's Message, which said, "Few studies will answer all of the questions surrounding a topic and most good studies will raise new ones—and sometimes they raise more questions than they answer" (Laub, 2012). My questions reflect the oftentimes delicate balancing required of evaluators as they navigate the political and cultural context of program evaluation. My questions include:

1. Is "trust but verify" an appropriate stance for evaluators or are these mutually exclusive concepts? Author Barton Swaim proposed they are mutually exclusive when he said, "If you trust, you won't insist on verifying, whereas if you insist on verifying, clearly you don't trust" (Swaim, 2016).
2. Is it feasible and appropriate to balance accountability and capacity-building in the same evaluation?
3. How do you conduct longer and more frequent visits to build trust and mitigate impression management considering the already steep costs of site visits?
4. What is the optimal makeup of site-visit teams in terms of content, evaluation, and context expertise?

Table 5.6. Participants Interviewed for the Study

Rima Al-Azar	Winston Allen	Jane Beattie
Chris Bentley	Eric Billiet	Sheila Brommel
Courtney Brown	Natalie Donahue	Wendy Erisman
Kari Foley	Bradley Hiller	Melanie Hwalek
Ben Jaques-Leslie	Tania Jarosewich	David Johnson
Nils Junge	Delia Kundin	Holly Lewandoski
Trish Link	Jan Luker	Ann Mavis
Brian McInerney	Marija Nashokovska	Corey Newhouse
Beatrice Pierre	Dana Powell Russell	Jessica Pugil
Maira Rosas-Lee	Nisha Sachdev	Linda Schrader
Libby Smith	James Storm	Katharine Sullivan
Timothy Sutfin	Joan Sykora	Michelle Tolbert
Tonya Van Tol	Cheryl Vanacora	Paul Waldhart
Susan Wolfe	Helene Woods	Jeanne Zimmer

5. How do you include the voices of beneficiaries without putting them "on display" for your site visit?

I hope this study provokes more questions and that you seek answers from your colleagues before your next site visit. My thanks go out to the individuals named in Table 5.6 for graciously contributing their time and thoughts to make this study possible.

References

Laub, J. (2012, March). Director's message. *NIJ Journal 269*. Retrieved from http://www.nij.gov/journals/269/pages/director.aspx

Neal, J. W., Neal, Z. P., Van Dyke, E., & Kornbluh, M. (2015). Expediting the analysis of qualitative data in evaluation: A procedure for the rapid identification of themes from audio recordings. *American Journal of Evaluation, 36*, 118–132.

Norris, A. R. (2011). Impression management: Considering cultural, social, and spiritual factors. *Inquiries Journal/Student Pulse, 3*(07). Retrieved from http://www.inquiriesjournal.com/a?id=553

Sobo, E. J., Simmes, D. R., & Landsverk, J. A. (2003). Rapid assessment with qualitative telephone interviews: Lessons from an evaluation of California's Healthy Families program & Medi-Cal for children. *American Journal of Evaluation, 24*, 399–408.

Swaim, B. (2016, March 11). "Trust, but verify": An untrustworthy political phrase. *The Washington Post*. Retrieved from https://www.washingtonpost.com/opinions/trust-but-verify-an-untrustworthy-political-phrase/2016/03/11/da32fb08-db3b-11e5-891a-4ed04f4213e8_story.html?utm_term=.acf695437ace

RANDI K. NELSON is the founder of Partners in Evaluation, LLC, an independent evaluation and training consulting firm, and adjunct faculty at the University of Minnesota.

Chapman Haynes, M. & Johnson, A. (2017). Training needs of site visitors. In R. K. Nelson & D. L. Roseland (Ed.), *Conducting and Using Evaluative Site Visits. New Directions for Evaluation, 156*, 75–82.

6

Training Needs of Site Visitors

Melissa Chapman Haynes, Ashley Johnson

Abstract

A recent "rumination" by Michael Quinn Patton focused on the critical role of the evaluator in the conduct of qualitative evaluation methods (Patton, 2015a). The importance of the evaluator in site visits is no less important. Although it has been proposed that site visits indeed constitute a methodology (Lawrenz, Keiser, & Lavoie, 2003), it is essential that the field develop expectations for training of site visitors that are appropriate to the context and purpose of the site visit. In this chapter we provide a working framework for the training needs of site visitors based on what we know from training for accreditation visits, the literature on the psychological development of expertise, and interviews with three novice site visitors. We hope future studies will be conducted that systematically examine and make explicit the need for high-quality training of evaluators for site visits beyond the context of accreditation. © 2017 Wiley Periodicals, Inc., and the American Evaluation Association.

"You don't know what you don't know." This apt phrase was the response of a newly trained site visitor during an interview about the nature of that training. This accreditation training provided her with self-paced on-line learning modules, in-person training with ample opportunities to apply and practice, followed by conducting site visits with a senior evaluator who had extensive experience. An overall theme was the importance of having a training process that involved multiple opportunities to learn from and be supported by knowledgeable others.

Although the literature and accumulated knowledge on high-quality training for site visitors is sparse, the one exception is training for accreditation site visits, which are conducted to evaluate compliance with a specified set of standards. Because of the high stakes nature of these visits, the process and quality measures for accreditation site visits are often quite explicit. To better understand the nature of this training, we conducted interviews with three newly trained site visitors for a well-known accreditation agency. These interviews led to the development of a suggested framework for site-visitor training beyond accreditation, based on the extensive psychological literature on the development of expertise.

What We Already Know: Examples of Site-Visitor Training

Most well-documented examples of site-visit training are, not surprisingly, for organizations that conduct site visits for accreditation purposes. For example, the American Psychological Association utilizes the Commission on Accreditation (CoA) to outline dimensions of quality for training. A 1-day workshop is conducted to provide both "didactic and experiential exposure of the 'Guidelines and Principles for Accreditation' and the role and function of the site visitor" (American Psychological Association, 2006). All new site visitors must attend this workshop, and experienced visitors need to attend this workshop once every 5 years. Specific training is also provided on the responsibilities for leading a site-visit team.

The Network of Schools of Public Policy, Affairs, and Administration (NASPAA) conducts trainings in person and online that include members of the Commission on Peer Review and Accreditation (COPRA) and NASPAA staff. There are 10 videos that have been created and put online to provide orientation to the site-visit process and the NASPAA standards. Most interestingly, NASPAA is explicit about the role of the site visitor, noting that persons or teams are "more like investigators ... you are validating their story." Explicit guidelines and expectations lay out how to minimize interruption of the routine of the program, the role of making evaluative judgments during the site visit, and how to take an approach that the program will put forth its best and that the site visitor should not assume the program is hiding something.

As a final example—also accreditation focused—the Commission on Accreditation of Athletic Training Education (CAATE) is explicit about the attitude, knowledge, and skills required of their site visitors. For attitude, the CAATE expectation is that the site visitor will have maturity, objectivity, diplomacy, dedication, professionalism, the need for self-initiative, understanding of the confidential nature of the task, a cooperative attitude, an analytic approach to the task, and necessary degrees of flexibility. The expected knowledge includes that of the content, of the field, and of prior evaluative work and reports of the organization being visited. Finally, the required skills of the site visitor include interviewing, interpersonal communications, self-expression, note-taking, maintaining objectivity, deductive reasoning and logical analysis, and ability to deal with "attitudinal problems/resistance to interviewing." Finally, the CAATE is explicit about when a site visitor will be dismissed. Site visitors are asked to sign a confidentiality statement and recognize that they can be dismissed for unprofessional behavior, for poor evaluations, or for inability to adhere to the established procedures. Dismissal will be communicated in writing. A "Ten Commandments for the Site-Visit Team" is provided, including advice such as "Don't Worship Sacred Cows," also known as do not succumb to the pressure of powerful institutions (Commission on Accreditation for Athletic Training, 2014–15).

A Proposed Framework for Training Based on the Psychological Development of Expertise

Over the past few decades an extensive literature has accumulated about the psychological development of expertise, defined as reliably high levels of knowledge, skill, or performance as compared with less-experienced individuals (Ericsson, 2006). There is consensus, based on the accumulated literature, that expertise is attained through deliberate practice and is not simply innate ability (Tashman, 2013). Of interest to our examination of the training of site visitors is the empirical work on the development of expertise with consideration of the sociocultural context such as the Model of Domain Learning, or MDL (Alexander, 2003). This approach focuses on the dynamic relationships between knowledge, strategic processing, and interest. What may be most interesting about MDL is that the dynamics among knowledge, strategic processing, and interest shift based on an individual's level of competence.

Cognitive and educational psychologists have studied experts and the development of expertise in a range of contexts, including teachers, chess players (Chase & Simon, 1973; de Groot, 1965), artists, and professional athletes (Ericsson, 2006). Although there are various theoretical models, there are some generally agreed upon takeaways about how one becomes an expert, which we can apply to a proposed framework for the training of site visitors.

The model of domain learning puts forth three levels of learning, instead of simply referring to the more extreme categories of novice and expert. The initial stage, acclimation, is when the individual's learning is mostly fact-based (e.g., declarative knowledge) and situational. An individual at the acclimation stage would have little experience with site visits and learning might be focused on surface-level strategies, such as knowing how to code a standardized rubric, or where to find a particular type of information. As the individual spends time in reflective practice that is focused on the domain, they will move into the second stage, which is competence. In this middle stage, the individual's knowledge contains some facts as well as some patterns, allowing them to use a combination of surface-level and deep processing strategies. And with continued deliberate practice an individual will obtain expertise or proficiency, where knowledge will become more of a process instead of mostly factual (procedural instead of declarative) and strategic processing will use deep processing strategies. Further, individual interest will increase and situational interest will decrease.

So how does one move through these stages to obtain a proficient or expert level of knowledge in a domain? Practice makes perfect is more than a saying. It is actually backed up with decades of research, though with the caveat that all types of practice are not equal. Deliberate practice is a specific type of practice where the individual is engaged in practice that requires attention (it is not passive), is at an appropriate level of difficulty, includes opportunities for immediate feedback, provides opportunities for making and correcting errors, and builds upon an individual's strengths while also working on their weaknesses (Ericsson, 2006, 2007). Expertise is obtained after 10 years or 10,000 hours of this specific type of deliberate practice, with a strong emphasis on the quality of practice being a vital component of developing expertise (Ericsson, 2003).

This chapter does not allow space for delving deep into the literature on expertise. However, we have extracted a few points that can be transferred from the literature, supported with examples from our interviews with newly trained site visitors, and our own experiences conducting and training site visitors in our evaluation practice.

Provide Opportunities for Learning and Feedback from "Expert" Site Visitors

During our interviews, the importance of doing site visits in teams with a senior-level or highly experienced individual emerged as an important and powerful learning opportunity. In our own practice, outside of accreditation site visits, we also engage in having a more experienced evaluation lead as one way of training less experienced site visitors. Conducting site visits in this manner, with opportunities for reflection and debriefing throughout the process, can support the development of less-experienced site visitors in multiple ways. Most obviously, this provides an opportunity for the less-experienced site visitor to gain experience without the pressure of being solely responsible for the planning, execution, and overall quality of the site visit. It can also provide opportunities for timely feedback and opportunities for questioning within the site-visit context, which produces a powerful learning opportunity.

The newly trained accreditation interviewees each had conducted their first site visit with a more senior site visitor. This accreditation process mandated that each site visit be conducted in pairs, led by an experienced site visitor. The interviewees indicated that the senior site visitor modeled behavior not learned during the online or in-person training sessions, such as being sensitive about when to ask questions (or not) and how to handle difficult personalities or tensions during the visit. Further, it was reported that the more-experienced site visitor noticed aspects of the site-visit context that the novice interviewee did not. For example, one newly trained site visitor noted that the senior site visitor told the novice visitor that the site-visit context was atypical, based on the senior site visitor's experience. This is something that the novice visitor wondered about but was not sure how to address; she reported learning a lot by watching the senior visitor address various concerns. Overall, the novice visitor reported that conducting the site visit helped to "put all of the pieces together" from prior trainings, and that this experience was "invaluable."

One Is the Loneliest Number

One lesson that Johnson, this chapter's second author, learned from implementing a train-the-trainer model for site visits at a small nonprofit was that new site visitors expressed feeling better going into and coming out of a site visit simply not having done it alone, even if the other person had equal inexperience. It should be noted that in this context all site visitors had completed training and had experience in relevant contexts, but not necessarily in program evaluation or in conducting site visits. A review of site-visit documentation demonstrated that pairs of site visitors produced better notes, were more likely to follow up on any actions that were needed after the visit, and more thoroughly completed the visit rubrics.

In addition, pairs or teams of newly trained or less-experienced site visitors can also provide a powerful learning opportunity. Recently trained site visitors can prepare and execute a site visit collaboratively, working together to ensure the visit's purpose is served, then collectively reflect on strengths, weaknesses and opportunities for improvement in future site-visit work. This type of shared learning experience may build visitors' confidence in their capacity to conduct a quality visit while leaving room for picking up where another may have less competence or knowledge. It produces shared learning and growth before, during, and after a site visit, ultimately serving as additional training, another opportunity to put new information and skills into action. Conducting site visits in pairs also increases the likelihood of site-visit success by leveraging the skills of each visitor.

Identify and Build Upon Strengths While Working on Weaknesses

We would be remiss if we did not note that this issue aligns well with the American Evaluation Association's task force's work on competencies, which is currently under way (see Stevahn, King, Ghere, & Minnema, 2005). Although there are not yet recommendations from this task force, prior work sheds light on some domains in which evaluators should be competent. For example, Chapman Haynes (this chapter's first author) uses an existing self-assessment in a graduate-level evaluation internship course (Stevahn, King, Ghere, & Minnema, 2004). Students respond to items within six competency categories at the beginning of the semester, identifying one or two areas they plan to focus on during their internship experience. Throughout the semester there are various reflective assignments and discussions related to these competencies. At the end of the semester students take the self-assessment a second time and reflect on their development (or lack of) within each of the competencies throughout the semester. Perhaps the most interesting takeaway from implementing this activity is the overall increase in self-awareness of the students throughout the semester, beyond any of the individual competency areas. Generally, students seem to have a broader picture of our field and what it takes to conduct evaluation and a realization of how much they have yet to learn.

Build Literature and Resources on Site Visits

It has been noted throughout this chapter, as well as in other recent publications (Patton, 2015a, 2015b), that there is a dearth of literature and guidance on site visits. Some preliminary work has been conducted on proposing site-visit standards (Patton, 2015b). These standards might be used as a basis for training, which would be somewhat analogous to the site-visit standards in place at many accreditation agencies. With accreditation, standards are typically used for the rating of sites. For the purpose of training site visitors, we might use standards in more of a meta sense, for evaluators conducting site visits to be meta-evaluated using standards. Such standards might also be useful for those who commission or use site visits as an indicator of quality.

Along with the site-visit standards proposed by Patton, the five components of the Program Evaluation Standards (Yarbrough, Shulha, Hopson, & Caruthers, 2011) might be considered as a basis for training, although there is certainly overlap between these two sets of standards. Patton's 10 proposed standards include having a competent evaluator who is trained in fieldwork (qualitative observation and interviewing specifically) as well as in the field of program evaluation, preparation prior to conducting the visit, engaged and considerate participation at the site during the visit, debriefing and feedback to key personnel at the site toward the end of the visit, review of the site-visit report by the personnel at the site, and follow-up with the site by the agency that commissioned the visit. The site-visit standards could certainly be used to guide evaluation commissioning agencies in what should be expected of a quality site visit and might guide the questions that are posed during site-visit follow-up conversations.

NEW DIRECTIONS FOR EVALUATION • DOI: 10.1002/ev

Reflection and Next Steps

Site visits, sometimes referred to as on-site reviews, occur in a myriad of contexts, with a matching range of requirements for the site visitor's knowledge, skills, attitudes, and adherence to various guiding standards. Site visits draw upon and overlap with other methodologies, such as observation, case study, and interviews, but constitute a unique methodology, given that the duration is shorter than case studies and includes a variety of other methods, depending on the context and purpose.

Of particular importance is understanding how training of site visitors does or does not occur to help site visitors exercise control in what they see, who they speak with, and the like, due to power dynamics and the concern that other self-reports by the organization may have painted a picture that is rosier than reality. Understanding how organizations train site visitors to be aware of this power differential would be a potentially useful contribution to our understanding of how to increase the quality of site visits. In addition to in-person, in situ training opportunities, how might we support students, colleagues, and our own learning with case examples, role playing, or building on what has been learned about this topic in other domains or professions?

In the first chapter of this volume, training of site visitors was one of the identified dimensions of the typology. The authors defined training to include the extent that site visitors are trained or have defined credentials (education and/or experience) prior to conducting the site visit. Four broad categories were proposed: no or little training or background; no training with some background; moderate training and background; and extensive training and background. What we propose in this chapter is that not all experience is or should be weighted equally. We should be mindful of specifying the type of experience and ensuring that training of site visitors provides opportunities for deliberate practice, learning from more experienced or proficient evaluators, opportunities to build and reflect on evaluator competencies, and adherence to specific standards of good practice.

Moving forward, it would be useful to disseminate exemplars of high-quality site-visit training beyond what occurs for accreditation site visits. Further, given how long it takes to develop proficiency (a decade!) site-visit-specific resources would be helpful as practitioners continue to deepen their understanding of this methodology. Such resources might be shared as part of the American Evaluation Association's Teaching of Evaluation Topical Interest Group (AEA TIG) or perhaps it is time to develop a new TIG that focuses on site visits.

References

Alexander, P. (2003). The development of expertise: The journey from acclimation to proficiency. *Educational Researcher, 32*, 10–14.

American Psychological Association. (2006). *Guidelines and principles for accreditation of programs in professional psychology (G&P)*. Retrieved from http://www.apa.org/ed/ accreditation/about/policies/guiding-principles.pdf

Chase, W. G., & Simon, H. A. (1973). The mind's eye in chess. In W. G. Chase (Ed.), *Visual information processing* (pp. 215–281). New York, NY: Academic Press.

Commission on Accreditation for Athletic Training. Site visitor handbook: 2014–15 site visits. Retrieved from http://caate.net/wp-content/uploads/2014/05/ Site-Visitor-Handbook-2014-2015.pdf

de Groot, A. (1965). *Thought and choice in chess*. The Hague, Netherlands: Mouton.

Ericsson, K. A. (2003). Development of elite performance and deliberate practice. In J. L. Starkes and K. A. Ericsson (Eds.), *Expert performance in sports: Advances in research on sports expertise* (pp. 49–83). Champagne, IL: Human Kinetics.

Ericsson, K. A. (2006). Protocol analysis and expert thought: Concurrent verbalizations of thinking during experts' performance on representative task. In K. A. Ericsson, N. Charness, P. Feltovich, & R. R. Hoffman (Eds.), *Cambridge handbook of expertise and expert performance* (pp. 223–242). Cambridge, UK: Cambridge University Press.

Ericsson, K. A. (2007). Deliberate practice and the modifiability of body and mind: Toward a science of the structure and acquisition of expert and elite performance. *International Journal of Sport Psychology*, 38, 4–34.

Lawrenz, F., Keiser, N., & Lavoie, B. (2003). Evaluative site visits: A methodological review. *American Journal of Evaluation*, 24, 341–452.

Patton, M. Q. (2015a). *Qualitative research and evaluation methods: Integrating theory and practice*. Thousand Oaks, CA: SAGE.

Patton, M. Q. (2015b). Evaluation in the field: The need for site visit standards. *American Journal of Evaluation*, 36, 444–460.

Stevahn, L., King, J., Ghere, G., & Minnema, J. (2004). *Essential competencies for program evaluators' self-assessment*. Retrieved from http://www.cehd.umn.edu/OLPD/ MESI/resources/ECPESelfAssessmentInstrument709.pdf

Stevahn, L., King, J. A., Ghere, G., & Minnema, J. (2005). Establishing essential competencies for program evaluators. *American Journal of Evaluation*, 26, 43–59.

Tashman, L. (2013). The development of expertise in performance: The role of memory, knowledge, learning, and practice. *Journal of Multidisciplinary Research*, 5(3), 33–48.

Yarbrough, D. B., Shulha, L. M., Hopson, R. K., & Caruthers, F. A. (2011). *The program evaluation standards: A guide for evaluators and evaluation users* (3rd ed.). Thousand Oaks, CA: SAGE.

Melissa Chapman Haynes is a senior evaluator at Professional Data Analysts in Minneapolis, MN.

Ashley Johnson is a senior program evaluator with Hennepin County's North-Point Health and Wellness Center's Innovation Group.

Patton, M. Q. (2017). Revised site-visit standards: A quality-assurance framework. In R. K. Nelson & D. L. Roseland (Eds.), *Conducting and Using Evaluative Site Visits. New Directions for Evaluation, 156*, 83–102.

7

Revised Site-Visit Standards: A Quality-Assurance Framework

Michael Quinn Patton (iD)

Abstract

Based on the chapters in this volume and feedback from others, this chapter presents a revised framework for site-visit standards. The framework, for the first time, uses a quality-assurance approach to distinguish minimum quality-control standards for site visits in addition to quality-enhancement principles aimed at ensuring excellence. The chapter concludes with a call to make evaluation fieldwork standards-based. © 2017 Wiley Periodicals, Inc., and the American Evaluation Association.

The Ongoing Evolution of Site-Visit Standards

This is how it's supposed to be when ideas evolve through professional interaction with colleagues and peer review. Revision follows revision and the work evolves. This chapter reports that evolution. Not completion. Not closure. But a new stage opening new possibilities for further understanding, inquiry, and evolution.

For years, while conducting training on qualitative evaluation, I have lamented the poor quality of many evaluation site visits. That led to a chapter in the *American Journal of Evaluation* proposing site-visit standards (Patton, 2015a). I received reactions and feedback from several people agreeing with the need for standards, but also suggesting some revisions and a need to widen the evidence and theory about evaluation site visits. Based on the feedback I received—and especially the insights from the chapters in this volume—I have revised the standards I proposed in previous writings (Patton, 2015a, 2015b). I have expanded the list of standards from 10 to 12, adding the new standards Interpersonal Competence and Cultural Competence. I have also revised the wording of several of the previously proposed standards. In so doing, I have created a new framework for site-visit standards that distinguishes levels of quality for each standard. The revised framework for site-visit standards also explicitly cites and connects to relevant standards that already inform the practice of evaluation. Finally, the revised framework makes explicit who is responsible for ensuring adherence to the standards. I begin by listing selected standards and examples of insights from chapters in this volume that elucidate and support that standard. I then present the revised framework.

Support for Existing Standards from Chapters

Standard 1. Evaluation Competence

Where the purpose of the site visit is evaluative, ensure that at least one team member has evaluation knowledge and credentials.

Chapter 1. Criterion for selection of evaluation site visitors varies widely. The extent to which site visitors are trained or have defined credentials in evaluation (education and/or experience) prior to conducting the site visit also varies greatly.

Chapter 3. The data collected through an evaluation site visit must be intimately tied to the intended use of the findings. In accreditation site visits, the standards that site reviewers are assigned are based on the knowledge and skills they have from where they work. The team leader matches the reviewers' strengths with the assignments to ensure the best available reviewer is doing a review of a standard that relates to the reviewer's background and strengths.

Chapter 4. It is possible and appropriate to assess prior experiences of potential site visitors for implementing evaluation site visits.

Chapter 5. Among those who said site visitors should have evaluation expertise defined it as having an advanced degree or extensive coursework in evaluation generally and in qualitative methods, specifically. An internal evaluator described desirable evaluation expertise as having "broad knowledge of program and policy evaluation and an analytical mind to systematically and logically address evaluation and data."

Chapter 6. Not all experience is or should be weighted equally. We should be mindful of specifying the type of experience and ensuring that training of site visitors provides opportunities for deliberate practice, learning from more experienced or proficient evaluators, opportunities to build and reflect on evaluator competencies, and adhere to specific standards of good practice.

NEW DIRECTIONS FOR EVALUATION • DOI: 10.1002/ev

Standard 2. Methodological Competence

Ensure that site-visit team members have skills and experience in observation and interviewing. Although general methodological competence is expected, methodological competences specific to the conduct of site visits and the specific purposes of a given site visit are needed.

Chapter 1. Methods competence needs to be matched to site-visit purpose.

Chapter 2. Incorporating other sources of data and information to supplement data collected during site visits will enhance research quality and affect credibility and utility.

Chapter 3. In accreditation visits, methods are externally directed to ensure credibility and accountability.

Chapter 4. An example of one evaluator's methodological competence is documented.

Chapter 5. An analytical mind—systematic and logical—is important; site visitors must be able to synthesize qualitative and quantitative data, and assimilate lots of new information and data quickly.

Chapter 6. Site visits draw upon and overlap with other methodologies, such as observation, case study, and interviews, but constitute a unique methodology.

Standard 3. Interpersonal Competence

Ensure that site-visit team members can interact respectfully and effectively with the diverse people they are likely to encounter during the site visit.

Chapter 1. The nature and extent of interpersonal engagement varies by type and purpose of the site visit.

Chapter 4. For site visitors, establishing rapport is important. They should attend to nonverbal and verbal cues and be sensitive to and adapt to characteristics of the people and groups at the site. Formation of relationships deepens the level of data that can be obtained, provides insight needed to understand and analyze the data, and informs the focus of the final evaluation. Being able to engage with those who are the experts (the people at the site), to understand what is being observed, provides invaluable insights. Bring humor, honesty, humility, and humanity to site visits.

Chapter 5. Interviewees highlighted the importance of interpersonal skills for conducting an effective site visit. These included having the ability to make people comfortable, being approachable and friendly, communicating diplomatically, and acting with humility and respect. People described respect as being aware of and appreciating the time people were giving to participate in the site visit. Some described interpersonal skills in terms of being "personable and compassionate," and others emphasized the need for site visitors to be "nonjudgmental"—to let site staff know you are interested in learning about their program rather than catching them making mistakes.

NEW DIRECTIONS FOR EVALUATION • DOI: 10.1002/ev

Chapter 6. Skills needed by the site visitor include interpersonal communications, self-expression, and ability to deal with "attitudinal problems/resistance to interviewing."

Standard 4. Cultural Competence

"A culturally competent evaluator is prepared to engage with diverse segments of communities to include cultural and contextual dimensions important to the evaluation. Culturally competent evaluators respect the cultures represented in the evaluation throughout the process" (American Evaluation Association, 2011, p. 1).

Chapter 1. Culture is a factor in defining the context for site visits; sensitivity to context and culture is critical.

Chapter 3. Discuss any cultural dynamics that should be considered prior to the site visit.

Chapter 4. In recruiting site visitors, assess experience in multicultural settings. Recognize and seek to understand how being culturally situated may influence a visit, how it influences those visited, and how it affects those who use the findings.

Chapter 5. Evaluators working in international development identified the need to work in teams of people with complementary skills that included knowledge of local conditions, cultures, and languages in addition to content and evaluation expertise. Other interviewees also identified cultural competence as a specific and essential skill of an effective site visitor. An internal evaluator said cultural competence "was too often lacking [and evaluators] need to be aware of [their] own biases about the population being served." An evaluator who had a particularly bad experience with a site visitor recounted his racist and sexist jokes that offended everyone on site, which interfered with the evaluation findings. One of the two evaluation commissioners said being culturally competent was important.

Chapter 6. Of interest to our examination of the training of site visitors is the empirical work that has examined the development of expertise with consideration of the sociocultural context.

Standard 5. Planning and Preparation

Site visitors should know enough about the site(s) being visited to conduct fieldwork appropriate to the purpose of the site visit.

Chapter 1. The higher the stakes, the more advance preparation, planning, and training are important. The time available for planning and implementing the site visit, ranging from expedited timelines to those which span an extended period, affects planning and preparation; it is too often the case that the timeline for planning and preparing for site visits is too short for adequate advance work.

Chapter 2. Too often, site visits are poorly planned and executed, or are not designed for a distinct purpose. The planning consideration that matters most is this question: "Does the use of site visits deliver unique value to whoever commissions the evaluation and to the site being visited?" If the answer is yes, then evaluators should proceed with additional planning considerations related to budgeting for the cost of site visits, the time to prepare for and conduct site visits, and other process-related considerations.

Chapter 3. Reviewer training is mandatory for accreditation site visits. The formal training for reviewers and team leaders includes, but is not limited to, reviewer roles and responsibilities, standards rating methodology, the use of professional judgment in the rating process, working as a team to develop consensus, and interviewing. Team leaders also receive additional training in establishing a site-visit schedule (formal interviews, program observation visits), managing the team, and managing site-visit logistics. Extensive planning and preparation are required.

Chapter 4. To be well prepared for the site visits, the site visitor spoke with the core program team and read key documents that informed what she needed to see and with whom she needed to speak.

Chapter 5. Evaluators and program staff alike noted the importance of preparing for a site visit well in advance of the actual visit. Preparation included planning for the logistics of the visit, giving notice of upcoming visits, developing protocols and agendas, and doing one's "homework" to learn as much as possible about the program and context before arriving on site.

Plan the visit. Evaluators said it was important to account for logistics and schedules to make most efficient use of their limited time on site. Logistics included things as pragmatic as knowing "where to park and what door to enter" at a school and knowing the school's guidelines and rules about visiting classrooms. Preparation was especially important for evaluators working far from home, because leaving a site to return at a more convenient time was not usually an option.

Chapter 6. Training before site visits is also an opportunity for planning and preparation.

Standard 6. Site Participation

People at the site should be engaged in planning and preparation for the site visit to minimize disruption to program activities and services to program beneficiaries.

Chapter 1. The nature of site engagement may range from those that are entirely directed externally with little engagement of the individuals on site beyond meetings or interviews or it may be highly collaborative and participatory. Accreditation visits tend to have less engagement with individuals at the site beyond observation of certain activities or programs in action or interviews with specified individuals. On the other hand, site visits that are conducted for the purposes of facilitating an activity toward

NEW DIRECTIONS FOR EVALUATION • DOI: 10.1002/ev

the development of logic models will be much more collaborative in nature. Those at the site may be involved with providing input on the individuals or groups that should be involved, and the design and implementation of activities on site. The nature of engagement is highly related to the purpose and to whether the actual process of asking people to engage in the site visit is intended to stimulate change in the program, intervention, or initiative.

Chapter 3. Leading up to the site visit, organizations undergo a lengthy and formal self-study process that typically takes 6–10 months to complete. During this period, they compare their practices against COA's standards, initiate new practices, or remediate self-identified deficiencies or gaps between current practices and the requirements of the standards. They also develop an evidentiary record that shows standards have been sufficiently implemented to justify earning accreditation. The formal self-study process ends approximately 6–8 weeks prior to the site visit. At the end of the self-study period, the organization submits a substantial number of documents to COA, which are collectively referred to as the organization's "self-study." To clarify, "self-study" refers to both this collection of documents and the self-evaluation process.

Chapter 4. Dysfunctional programs make collaboration difficult to impossible. Collaboration requires a certain level of competence, commitment, and engagement on the program end, including a program's board and senior staff.

Chapter 5. Developing and providing program sites with an agenda that includes the "who, what, when, where, why, and how" of an upcoming visit was an important aspect of planning. Evaluators described the need to be "transparent" to reduce program stakeholders' fears about what would happen during a site visit and to keep them from feeling "ambushed." International evaluators said it was often too difficult to get to remote sites without providing notice to the program site liaisons in advance of the visit. Program staff appreciated getting notified in advance so they could "be prepared and have the right people on hand" so they could efficiently answer the evaluator's questions and not waste the time of program stakeholders waiting to be interviewed. However, one site coordinator said it was also important for evaluators to be able to "drop in" on a program without notice in cases where fraud was suspected.

Chapter 6. Of particular importance is understanding how training of site visitors does or does not occur to help site visitors exercise control in what they see, who they speak with, and being prepared to deal with the power dynamics that arise between evaluators and program staff.

Space does not allow for presentation of the supporting evidence from all the chapters for all 10 standards. The preceding examples provide a sense of the process I used in drawing on the chapters to revise the site-visit standards framework. I invite readers to do their own analysis for the remaining six standards. I now turn to the revised standards.

NEW DIRECTIONS FOR EVALUATION • DOI: 10.1002/ev

A New Framework for Site-Visit Standards

The new framework for site-visit standards uses the classic distinction in quality assurance between quality control and quality enhancement. *Quality control* focuses on standardized and universal *minimum standards* necessary for adequate functioning. Quality-control standards are like well-formulated goals: clear, specific, and measurable. *Quality enhancement*, in contrast, concerns going beyond the minimum to strive for excellence. *Excellence* involves attention and adaptation to context, professional judgment, and primarily qualitative data to inform and support rendering judgments of quality. The revised framework also explicitly cites and connects to relevant standards that already inform the practice of evaluation. Finally, the revised framework makes explicit who is responsible for ensuring adherence to standards. Table 7.1 presents the new framework. The principles in the second column of Table 7.1) (Excellence Principles) are in addition to minimums described in the first column (Minimum Threshold), not substitutes. The Editors' introduction to this volume includes a condensed version of the original standards.

Conclusion: Make Your Evaluation Work Standards-Focused

This volume documents the importance and dominance of site visits as an evaluation method. Determining quality standards for evaluation site visits is but an initial step toward increasing excellence in fieldwork. To have an effect, the standards must be followed in commissioning, conducting, and reporting site visits. The purpose of enhancing quality is not an end in itself, but increases the validity, value, credibility, and, ultimately, the utility of evaluation site visits.

I am regularly asked who should adopt these site-visit standards. Should they be brought before professional evaluation associations for study and potential adaptation and adoption? My response is this: If you are involved in evaluation site visits, whether as a funder, designer, site visitor, or object of site visits, *you can choose to adopt and follow these standards now*. Do not wait for the blessing of some official evaluation organization or professional association. Do not look to others. Look to what is right to do in your own setting. Make this a bottom-up movement toward enhanced site-visit quality. In whatever role you find yourself, with whatever power your knowledge, experience, and position affords you, *take a stand on standards*. Use the ones offered here if they align with your values. Adapt them to fit your situation and priorities, if need be. What we have proposed here is not the final word. It is a framework of possibilities. The question is, what standards will guide *your* evaluation fieldwork? If not these, then generate your own. What is not acceptable is to proceed without standards. Make your evaluation work, including site visits, standards based. That is the purpose, invitation, challenge, and vision of this volume.

NEW DIRECTIONS FOR EVALUATION • DOI: 10.1002/ev

Table 7.1. Revised Proposed Standards for Quality Site Visits: A Framework for Increasing Professionalism, Credibility, and Utility

Standard 1. Documented Evaluation Competence of Site Visitors. Where the Purpose of the Site Visit Is Evaluative, Ensure That at Least One Team Member Has Evaluation Knowledge and Credentials.

Minimum Threshold: Quality Control Mandates (Rules)	*Excellence Principles for Quality Enhancement*	*Whose Responsibility*	*Other Relevant and Supporting Standards*
(a) Documentation of specific evaluation knowledge, training, and professional evaluation involvement of potential site visitors (b) Relevant evaluation experiences documented and assessed (c) Knowledge of evaluation standards and guiding principles	Evaluation site visitor: (a) Active in the evaluation profession, e.g., member of an evaluation association, attends evaluation conferences (b) Knows classic evaluation literature (c) Reads current evaluation journals and books (d) Advanced training in evaluation (e) An experienced evaluator chairs the evaluation site-visit team	Commissioners and funders of site visits; those who write terms of reference and select the site-visit team	(a) AEA Guiding Principle on Evaluator Competency: Principle B (American Evaluation Association, 2003) (b) Competencies for Canadian evaluators adapted from work by Stevahn, King, Ghere, and Minnema (2005) and King, Stevahn, Ghere, and Minnema (2001)

(Continued)

Table 7.1. Continued

Standard 2. Methodological Competence. Ensure That Site-Visit Team Members Have Skills and Experience in Observation and Interviewing. Although General Methodological Competence Is Expected, Methodological Competences Specific to the Conduct of Site Visits and the Specific Purposes of a Site Visit Are Needed.

Minimum Threshold	Excellence Principles	Responsibility	Other Standards
(a) Documentation of specific requisite methodological skills on curriculum vitae and resumes	(a) Review examples of site visitors' prior reports for quality.	(a) Commissioners and funders of site visits; site-visit team leader	(a) AEA Guiding Principle on Systematic, Data-Based Inquiry: Principle A (American Evaluation Association, 2003)
(b) Relevant experiences documented	(b) Confirm references regarding methods competence.		(b) AEA Guiding Principle on Evaluator Competence: Principle B (American Evaluation Association, 2003)
	(c) Conduct a selection interview to gauge skills.		(c) OECD/DAC standard on selection of methodology (Standard 2.8) (OECD/DAC, 2010).
	(d) Identify and ensure the specific skills needed for the type, duration, focus, and stakes of the site visits.		(d) Competencies for Canadian Evaluators adapted from work by King et al. (2001): *Technical Practice Competencies* (No. 2)
			(e) Joint Committee Accuracy Standards (Yarbrough, Shulha, Hopson, & Caruthers, 2011)

(Continued)

Table 7.1. Continued

Standard 3. Interpersonal Competence. Ensure That Site-Visit Team Members Can Interact Respectfully and Effectively With the Diverse People They Are Likely to Encounter During the Site Visit.

Minimum Threshold	Excellence Principles	Responsibility	Other Standards
(a) Self-reports and reflective practice offered by potential site visitors (b) Written statement on approach to and perspective on interpersonal competence	(a) Solicit examples of interpersonal challenges faced and how handled. (b) Confirm references regarding interpersonal competence. (c) Conduct a selection interview to gauge interpersonal demeanor and skills. (d) Identify and ensure the specific interpersonal skills needed for the type, duration, focus, and stakes of the site visits to be conducted.	(a) Commissioners and funders of site visits (b) Site-visit team leader	(a) Competencies for Canadian Evaluators adapted from work by King et al. (2001): *Technical Practice Competencies* (No. 2) (b) AEA Guiding Principle on Respect for People (American Evaluation Association, 2003) (c) Interactive Evaluation Principles (King & Stevahn, 2015)

(Continued)

Table 7.1. Continued

Standard 4. Cultural Competence: "*A Culturally Competent Evaluator Is Prepared to Engage With Diverse Segments of Communities to Include Cultural and Contextual Dimensions Important to the Evaluation. Culturally Competent Evaluators Respect the Cultures Represented in the Evaluation Throughout the Process*" *(American Evaluation Association, 2011, Cultural Competence statement, p. 1).*

Minimum Threshold	Excellence Principles	Responsibility	Other Standards
(a) Self-reports and reflective practice offered by potential site visitors	(a) Solicit examples of cultural challenges faced and how handled.	(a) Commissioners and funders of site visits	(a) American Evaluation Association (2011)
(b) Written statement on approach to and perspective on cultural competence	(b) Confirm references regarding cultural competence.	(b) Site-visit team leader	(b) Defining an indigenous evaluation framework (LaFrance & Mekinak, 2010)
	(c) Conduct selection interviews to gauge cultural sensitivity; identify and ensure the specific cultural competencies needed for the type, duration, focus, and stakes of site visits.		

(Continued)

Table 7.1. Continued

Standard 5. *Planning and Preparation. Site Visitors Should Know Enough About the Site(s) Being Visited to Conduct Fieldwork Appropriate to the Purpose of the Site Visit.*

Minimum Threshold	Excellence Principles	Responsibility	Other Standards
In advance of the site visit, the site visitor(s) should be provided (a) Briefing materials about the site(s) (b) Complete program documentation (c) Clear scope of work	Train site visitors: Readings are rarely sufficient for advance preparation, especially where a site-visit team is being formed. For quality and consistency of field work, provide formal training.	(a) Commissioners and funders of site visits (b) Team members request (demand) adequate training to ensure quality performance.	(a) The Council on Accreditation's (COA) accreditation site-visit process (Council on Accreditation, 2016) (b) Commission on Accreditation of Athletic Training Education (CAATE)

(Continued)

Table 7.1. Continued

Standard 6. Site Participation. People at the Site Should Be Engaged in Planning and Preparation for the Site Visit to Minimize Disruption to Program Activities and Services to Program Beneficiaries.

Minimum Threshold	Excellence Principles	Responsibility	Other Standards
People at the site are fully informed in advance of the purpose, duration, team composition, data-collection methods, and schedule of the site visit. This information is provided sufficiently far in advance to permit clarifying questions to be asked and logistics to be arranged.	(a) People at the site participate in designing the site visit. Based on the site-visit purpose and stakes, the site visit is collaboratively designed, interactive, co-created, and utilization focused. (b) Be prepared to deal with power dynamics in the interactions between evaluation site visitors and program staff.	(a) Commissioners and funders of site visits (b) Team members request (demand) the opportunity to make the site visit utilization focused. (c) Programs should expect (demand) site visits be utilization focused and they have the opportunity to be considered primary intended users as appropriate to the fieldwork's purpose.	(a) Joint Committee Utility Standards (Yarbrough et al. 2011) (b) Utilization-Focused Evaluation Checklist (Patton, 2012) (c) Interactive Evaluation Principles (King & Stevahn, 2015) (d) Collaborative evaluation principles (Cousins, Shulha, Whitmore, Al Hudib & Gilbert, 2016)

(Continued)

Table 7.1. Continued

Standard 7. Do No Harm. Site Visits Are Not Benign. The Stakes Can Be High. People Can Be Put at Risk. Programs Can Be Put at Risk.

Minimum Threshold	Excellence Principles	Responsibility	Other Standards
Provide ethical guidelines to site visitors.	*Train site visitors in ethical guidelines.*	(a) Commissioners and funders of site visits (b) Team leaders	(a) Ethical standards of relevant disciplines like social work, psychology, anthropology, and sociology (b) Joint Committee Propriety Standards (Yarbrough et al., 2011) (c) Evaluation professional association ethical standards

(Continued)

Table 7.1. **Continued**

Standard 8. Credible Fieldwork. Although Those at the Site Should Be Involved and Informed, They Should Not Control the Information Collection in Ways That Undermine, Significantly Limit, or Corrupt the Inquiry.

Minimum threshold	Excellence Principles	Responsibility	Other Standards
(a) Negotiate access to needed data, documents, and people in advance of the site visit. (b) Establish and follow protocols for data collection that ensure the integrity, quality, and credibility of the fieldwork, and thus the evaluation findings.	(a) Work with program staff being visited to help them understand and appreciate how data must be collected to ensure the integrity, quality, and credibility of the fieldwork, and evaluation findings. (b) For high-stakes site visits, conduct an independent meta-evaluation to evaluate data-collection quality.	Evaluation site visitors	(a) Joint Committee Standard on Accuracy and Accountability; meta-evaluation (Yarbrough et al., 2011) (b) AEA Guiding Principle on Systematic Inquiry (American Evaluation Association, 2003)

(Continued)

Table 7.1. Continued

Standard 9. Neutrality. An Evaluator Conducting Fieldwork Should Not Have a Preformed Position on the Intervention or the Intervention Model. Openness to What the Data Reveal Is Essential but Cannot Be Assumed.

Minimum Threshold	Excellence Principles	Responsibility	Other Standards
Site visitors sign a statement ensuring no conflicts of interest and disclosing any known predispositions or biases that might affect the capacity to render fair and impartial judgments.	(a) Site-visit preparation and training includes examination of chapters that might arise that would threaten neutrality. (b) Any interactions during the site visit that would raise concerns about neutrality are included in report.	(a) Commissioners and funders of site visits (b) Team leaders (c) Team members (d) Program staff providing data to site visitors	(a) Independent Evaluation Group (IEG, World Bank) evaluation principles (Independent Evaluation Group, 2015) (b) AEA Guiding Principle on Integrity and Honesty (American Evaluation Association, 2003)

(Continued)

Table 7.1. Continued

Standard 10. Debriefing and Feedback. Before Departing From the Site Visit (Fieldwork), Some Appropriate Form of Debrief and Feedback Should Be Provided to Key People at the Site.

Minimum Threshold	Excellence Principles	Responsibility	Other Standards
Ensure a predeparture meeting with key people at the site to review how the site visit went, present initial findings, if appropriate, and explain next steps (e.g., what kind of report will follow, when, and in what form, with what opportunity for local review and response).	(a) Plan for and engage in a substantive dialogue about site-visit processes and findings. (b) Ensure opportunities for key people at the site to review findings and respond.	(a) Commissioners and funders of site visits (b) Team leaders (c) Team members (d) Program staff providing data to site visitors	Qualitative standards on fieldwork, feedback, and check-ins with people observed, interviewed, and reported on (Patton, 2015a, Chapters 6 and 7)

(Continued)

Table 7.1. Continued

Standard 11. Site Review: Those at the Site Should Have an Opportunity to Respond in a Timely Way to Site Visitors' Reports, to Correct Errors, and Provide an Alternative Perspective on Findings and Judgments, if Necessary.

Minimum Threshold	Excellence Principles	Responsibility	Other standards
Key people at sites visited receive the report and are offered an opportunity to respond within a reasonable time period.	(a) Arrange and ensure interactions and dialogue between site visitors, key people at the site visited, and those who commissioned the site visit. (b) Provide adequate time and resources during and after the visit for review, feedback, and dialogue.	(a) Commissioners and funders of site visits (b) Team leaders (c) Team members (d) Program staff providing data to site visitors	(a) The Council on Accreditation's accreditation site-visit process (Council on Accreditation, 2016) (b) Utilization-focused reporting principles (Patton, 2012, Chapter 13, Step 14)

(Continued)

Table 7.1. Continued

Standard 12. Follow-Up. The Agency Commissioning the Site Visit Should Follow Up to Assess the Quality of the Site Visit From the Perspective of the Locals on Site. The Site-Visit Team Should Know in Advance that Such a Follow-Up Assessment Will Take Place.

Minimum Threshold	Excellence Principles	Responsibility	Other Standards
Survey sent to key people at the site following the site visit soliciting overall reactions	Interviews and dialogue with key people at the site following the site visit, soliciting overall reactions and offering an opportunity for dialogue and learning	(a) Commissioners and funders of site visits (b) Team leaders (c) Team members (d) Program staff providing data to site visitors	(a) OECD/DAC Principles on evaluation follow-up (OECD/DAC, 2012) (b) The Council on Accreditation's accreditation site-visit process (Council on Accreditation, 2016)

References

American Evaluation Association. (2003). *Guiding principles of evaluators*. Retrieved from http://www.eval.org/p/cm/ld/fid=51

American Evaluation Association. (2011). *Public statement on cultural competence in evaluation*. Fairhaven, MA: Author. Retrieved from www.eval.org

Council on Accreditation. (2016). *About COA*. Retrieved from http://coanet.org/about/about-coa

Cousins, J. B., Shulha, L. M., Whitmore, E., Al Hudib, H., & Gilbert, N. (2016). How do evaluators differentiate successful from less-than-successful experiences with collaborative approaches to evaluation? *Evaluation Review, 40*, 3–28.

Independent Evaluation Group. (2015). *Evaluation standards*. Washington, DC: The World Bank. Retrieved from https://ieg.worldbankgroup.org/evaluation-principles-and-standards

King, J. A., & Stevahn, L. (2013). *Interactive evaluation practice: Mastering the interpersonal dynamics of program evaluation*. Thousand Oaks, CA: Sage.

King, J. A., Stevahn, L., Ghere, G., & Minnema, J. (2001). Toward a taxonomy of essential evaluator competencies. *American Journal of Evaluation, 22*, 229–247.

La France, J., & Mekinak, J. (2010). Reframing evaluation: Defining an indigenous evaluation framework. *The Canadian Journal of Program Evaluation, 23*, 13–31.

OECD/DAC. (2010). *Quality standards for development evaluation*. Retrieved from http://www.oecd.org/development/evaluation/qualitystandards.pdf

Patton, M. Q. (2012). *Essentials of utilization-focused evaluation*. Los Angeles, CA: Sage.

Patton, M. Q. (2015a). *Qualitative research & evaluation methods* (4th ed.). Los Angeles, CA: Sage.

Patton, M. Q. (2015b). Evaluation in the field: The need for site visit standards. *American Journal of Evaluation, 36*, 444–460.

Stevahn, L., King, J. A., Ghere, G., & Minnema, J. (2005). Establishing essential competencies for program evaluators. *American Journal of Evaluation, 26*, 43–59.

Yarbrough, D. B., Shulha, L. M., Hopson, R. K., & Caruthers, F. A. (2011). *The program evaluation standards: A guide for evaluators and evaluation users* (3rd ed.). Thousand Oaks, CA: Sage.

MICHAEL QUINN PATTON, *an independent evaluation consultant and author of eight major evaluation books, including* Developmental Evaluation *and* Principles-Focused Evaluation, *is based in Saint Paul, Minnesota, where he partners with his daughter, Charmagne Campbell-Patton, in their evaluation business, Utilization-Focused Evaluation.*

INDEX